D0968594

An Owl Came to Stay

An Owl Came to Stay

CLAIRE ROME

With illustrations by the author

CROWN PUBLISHERS, INC.
NEW YORK

55002 [redacted]

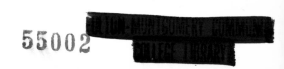

First published
1979 by
Paul Elek Ltd
54–58 Caledonian Road, London N1 9RN

First published in the U.S.A. 1980 by Crown Publishers, Inc.

Copyright © Claire Rome 1979

All rights reserved. No part of this publication
may be reproduced, stored in a retrieval system
or transmitted, in any form or by any means,
electronic, mechanical, photocopying, recording
or otherwise, without the prior permission of
the publishers.

ISBN 0 517 539802

Library of Congress Catalog Card Number: 79–2473

Printed in Great Britain by
Unwin Brothers Limited
The Gresham Press, Old Woking, Surrey
A member of the Staples Printing Group

To Chippy, without whose help this book would have been finished in half the time. And to Josephine and John.

Contents

Introduction

I set out to write this book partly to blow away a few cobwebs, and partly to share my experience with others; but mainly because I feel there is a lot about owls that scientific study and textbooks have missed out, things that only very close observation and sympathy with the living bird can reveal. Also, these learned writings are all from man's point of view. I want to tell about owls, the tawny in particular, from actually sharing their lives, to give a closer, 'owl's eye view'.

Most folk are daytime people and don't want to know much about what goes on in the darkness outside well lit city streets. Even in the country there are not many who would choose to go walking alone in the woods at night for pleasure. But I have met others who, like myself, prefer the night. It is not just that the hours of darkness are more restful after the stress and rush of work. No, it's far more than this: something basic in one's makeup, something almost primitive, deep rooted in the very depths of one's being, almost as though at dusk a switch turns one on to full alertness. Some people feel more at home in the hours of darkness than at any time during the day. I have always felt that it is such a pity that we should have to be fast asleep and miss the beauty of the earth lying still and tranquil under the light of the moon. Moonlight hides the crude and ugly, blending all with the flowing softness of the land. I envy the owls their design for darkness. I hope I have been able to lift the corner of the dark veil and show a little of what goes on in the life of these fascinating creatures.

I would like to express my sincere thanks to the Publishers for their help and encouragement in putting this book together.

Claire Rome
Sturminster Newton, Dorset

1

Wolly

The sun is shining, the lawns are cut, and among the spring flowers small birds are searching for nesting material. But they keep a safe distance from the studio window where I work, because as I write this there is an owl sitting on my shoulder. He is in fact the fourth of his kind who has taken it as his right to use me as a mobile perch.

It all started about six years ago, on a day in late spring very similar to this. I had been making a series of drawings of hawks and eagles, and had gone to London to return a case of stuffed birds lent to me by a friend. As we sat talking, he suddenly said, 'I've got something that might interest you.' Leaving the room, he was soon back to place in my lap . . . a baby owl. It was so sudden, so unexpected, that all I could do was gaze at the little creature, hardly daring to believe my eyes. As if coming from a long way off, I heard my friend's voice telling me how this chick had been found by some boys playing in a nearby park; how it had been under his care for two weeks, but now he had a problem on his hands. Owls and an office in town don't mix. As the chick was now big enough to start flying, could I suggest what might be done? The little chap on my lap didn't move. With strong claws gripping my fingers, his great dark eyes never left mine.

I thought furiously for a minute. I wondered . . . could it be done? Could I raise him and eventually turn him back to the wild?

'Not possible,' said my friend. 'Couldn't be done. But if you were to take him he would be better off with trees to look at than high-rise buildings.'

The owlet still looked up into my face, and right then I was sunk, almost without trace, drowned in that piteous entreaty for someone, anyone, *me*, to take him away from there; away to where there was peace, and the sight of at least one tree. Right there and then I made him a silent promise: if it were possible, one day he would go back to his rightful heritage in the wild woods.

A cardboard box was produced, holes punched in it for air, and the baby owl carefully inserted to begin the long journey home to the West country.

John met me at the station with the car, and on the twelve mile journey home no sound came from the box. Owlet had nothing to say at that time—nor did he when I tenderly extracted him from his little world of darkness to sit once more on my hand. But he had the good sense to turn the full power of those great dark eyes on John this time. It took just a little longer than one split second to sink him too, and all possible objection that could have arisen to this new addition to the family was silenced before it arose, then and forever.

For a first feed we mixed soft feathers from a down pillow (burst open by an over-exuberant niece on a recent visit) with small pieces of raw beef, warmed slightly in the oven to take the chill off. Owlet made short work of a meal that ought to have foundered a full grown buzzard, and subsided into well-stuffed content, still on my hand, still saying nothing. Almost too sleepy to notice much, he was carried out to the studio. We laid newspapers in a corner and put a perch made out of a log on top. When he was given to me the owlet was 'jessed', that is, leather straps were fastened onto his legs to prevent him flying off his perch in the office and perhaps hurting himself. I removed the jesses from around each of his legs, parked him on his log and left him to snooze off his meal in peace.

Our three hundred year old cottage, hidden away from the rest of the village, is built of stone, with walls nearly two feet thick. Originally it was thatched, but since the First World War its steeply pitched roof has been clad in heavy slates. At one end there was a shed which had originally been a stable; it was also built of stone, with a sloping roof. This, when we first saw it, was a repository for all sorts of junk stored right up to its ceiling—corn bins, rolls of wire netting, packing cases, brass bedsteads, coal, firewood, old sacks, broken tools and odd bits of furniture. It took nine tractor trailer-loads to clear it out, and it was only then that we saw that it had a good concrete floor and was dry and damp free. For the first few years we used it for storing coal. Then, from the sale of one of my paintings, I decided to have it converted into a studio. The walls were insulated and lined, a big storage cupboard built, and the front wall facing south to the garden taken out and replaced with plate-glass windows and a door, and the whole area was painted white inside. It made a room about twenty feet by seventeen feet, and a wonderful place to work in. The only snag was that in Dorset they had a habit of building a huge chimney at one end of the house and then resting the end of the roof on it. This meant that we could not make a way through from the studio into the house, so one has to go out of the garden door and along the front of the house to get indoors. A bit awkward in rain or snow, but we soon got used to that. We had no idea, in those early days, that this studio was to become 'home' for a succession of young owls!

The owlet slept the sleep of all tiny well-fed things for an hour, then woke to the fact that the world around had stopped moving and making strange sounds, and that here was a New Place.

First he gave it the once-over from his perch, bobbing about and swivelling his head to get a good look at everything from floor to ceiling. Then he hopped off the log and proceeded on a tour of close inspection. Pottering around the floor, he took his time, tapping things with his beak, peering behind canvases and drawing boards stacked against the walls and finally disappearing under the cover of the studio couch. All was quiet for a while except for various rustlings and thumps as he climbed about over portfolios and odds and ends that I keep there. At last he emerged, and apparently reassured that nothing lurked in the corners, he toddled across to me, and climbing up onto my lap, lay down on his side, and in a few seconds was fast asleep.

This little bundle of greyish feathers was a tawny owl about five weeks old, and we named him Wolly. He had an almost insatiable appetite and a sense of curiosity to match. Everything around him had to be examined, beak-tested, jumped on or flown at. Oh yes, he could already fly strongly. And he had a *voice*. At meal times a *loud voice*. I could hear his penetrating, high-pitched squeals and shrieks from the kitchen at the other end of the house when I was preparing his food. Soon log-on-the-floor was too low, so it was moved to the top of a cupboard, then to the top of the bookcase. But still it was not a private enough place for him. So, getting saw and hammer, I fixed him a wide shelf high up in the darkest corner, about a foot below the ceiling. Not an easy thing to do when he would insist on helping, first from my shoulder, then offering advice and comment from the top of my head. However, between us we finally got the job done to his satisfaction, and he flew up to give the room another inspection from this new vantage point. He made several swooping dives from there for a few minutes, then back to lie down and rest, a contented expression on the little face poking over the edge.

In the weeks that followed he thrived and grew. Oh, how he grew! We could almost watch him getting bigger every minute. He was always fed at dusk. At first he came to my hand or sat on my lap to be fed, but soon his food was put on a broad wooden plank on top of the bookcase, from which he could feed himself. In addition to the mice that we and the cat caught for him, he had beef, chicken-neck, liver, heart, calcium tablets, vitamin drops . . . you name it . . . he ate it. He stole the sardines from my lunchtime sandwiches; he devoured tinned salmon and tunnyfish too, along with bits of crust and anything else that he could get his beak into. Anything I ate, he had to sample, not because he was hungry, but just because I had it. If anyone were foolhardy enough to bring a plate with food on it into the studio, it was a foregone conclusion that sooner rather than later one could expect that flying appetite to dive right into the middle of it!

He had to be given, nay, loudly demanded, bits of paper and cloth to tear up. Discovering where the box of face-tissues was kept, he helped himself, tearing them to shreds. He tore the spines off paperback books, pulled the underfelt from the carpet, ripped the fringe off the couch cover, and even had a go at the curtains, but luckily they resisted his strong beak. He stole my pencils and brushes, fell into the paint, and in general nothing was safe from his attentions ... least of all me. I got flown at, landed on, shrieked at, and had my hair preened until I looked as though I had just been for a quiet stroll in a force eight gale.

I got into the habit of spending a few nights each week sleeping out in the studio with him, as I wanted to see just what a young owl did at night when he became fully alert. I might have known. Although he

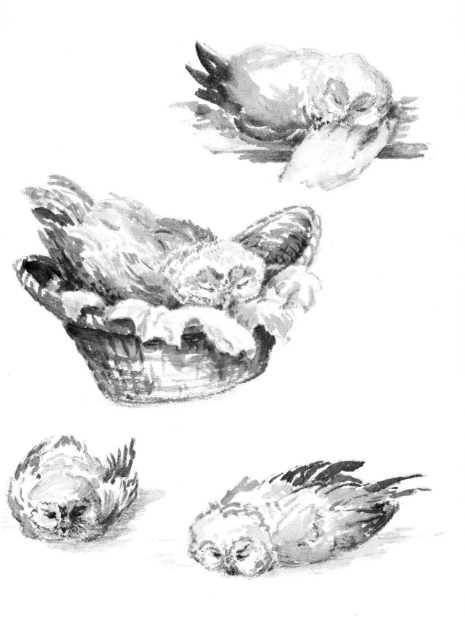

was active during the day he was even more so after dark, and thought it wonderful to have me there to play with. But as he slept soundly from about one a.m. till dawn, my sleep wasn't too restricted, and being with him cemented the already close bond between us.

While he was still young, there was nothing that Wolly liked better than to be taken into the sitting room when guests were there in the evenings. He was a Smash Hit and instant conversation stopper. From his perch on my knee he would survey the assembled company. Stretching a wing was greeted with 'Oh, isn't he beautiful', while a bit of head-bobbing earned further admiration. Being a complete ham he was quick to exploit the situation. Knowing that he had everyone's rapt attention, it was more than I dared do to stop him as he swaggered his way slowly across the carpet, and up via chairback and couch, to the top of the television set. More posing, to make sure that all eyes were still on him, and then a quick sideways glide toward a big bowl of flowers that stood nearby. A quick nip from his beak and a flower bit the dust. Admiring giggles spurred him on, another and another flower hit the floor; then, having demolished the nearest and getting really warmed to his job, he jumped boldly in with both feet. Water, flowers and bits of oasis were soon flying in all directions. But enough is enough, and amid a chorus of regret from his admirers I had to carry one protesting owl back to the studio again, before he completely wrecked the place.

As he grew he was shedding his baby feathers. The whole place was awash with them. In the mornings, the floor of my normally tidy studio resembled nothing so much as a disaster area: the aftermath of where a combination cyclone of paper and feather-storm had passed. And amid all the debris sat Wolly, with a smug, self-satisfied look on his face, watching while I cleared it all up.

He discovered the basket in which I keep the clothes pegs, and promptly adopted it as his day-bed. But as he was growing so fast, soon it was not big enough, and he looked for a more suitable place. The summer days were hot, and the curtain by my table was drawn to keep out the glare of the sun. Wolly cat-walked along the window sill and inspected this cool spot. He pushed the curtain until it bulged over the sill, then stepping into the hammock he had made, lay down to take full advantage of any passing breeze. So each morning I had to pin the material firmly to the sill in case he fell out, and he would wait until everything was fixed to his satisfaction before climbing in for a siesta.

During the hot August days he would be perched on top of the open door that led out into the garden, but when it got really hot he liked to sit directly in the

draught of the electric fan, obviously finding its low hum very soothing, for I was soon asked what I thought I was doing with *his* fan when I switched it off.

Early in his young life, Wolly discovered the joys of taking a bath. First he would drink, letting the water run down his throat, savouring each drop like a wine-taster. Then he would contemplate the water for a while, fluffing and rousing his feathers in anticipation. After a few minutes of this he would step daintily in and sit down with a rather surprised expression on his face. Sometimes, dispensing with the preliminaries, he would charge over, and taking a wild leap, land with a terrific splash right in the middle of the bath, sending showers of water all over the floor. Ducking his head, with a wriggling, swimming motion he would then throw the water over his back and wings. But on more exuberant occasions, he would slide about, often falling on his side, amid shrieks and squeaks of pleasure. But whatever the method, his ablutions were not over until there was no more water left in the bath—but much over the surrounding landscape! Then, having finished, he would what can only be described as 'scruttle' up and down on the towel provided to soak up spilled water, and dry himself off. And this, I thought with misgivings, is the owl I'm supposed to turn back to the wild. But he was happy and content, and that was all that mattered for the moment.

Owls, being creatures of the night, need to get their share of Vitamin D, and so take a sunbath whenever they can. A favourite place for the wild owls seems to be on the bales in the fields after the hay has been cut, and I have often seen them there on summer mornings. Wolly found that the ideal place was on my drawing board, but as this is propped up at an angle he kept sliding off—until we solved the problem together. I had to fold my arms across it, and when he was securely anchored against me, he would turn his face to the sun and luxuriate in the warmth. Gradually his wings would spread out to reveal the full beauty of their intricate patterning, the almost transparent tail fanning out until every feather was exposed to the health-giving light. There he would stay for perhaps a quarter of an hour in the full sun, while I got hotter and hotter, not daring to disturb him until he had had enough. Then he would fly to the top of the door, and with wings drooping and throat panting, complain that now he was too hot. There was only one thing to do . . . fan him with a newspaper until he cooled down!

One day he found that the wide concrete step to the studio door made another good spot for a sunbath. He was so absorbed with sitting in the light that at first I'm sure he didn't realize he was actually outside. It wasn't until a few minutes after his sunbath that the fact dawned on him. He went back for another look at the garden from this new-found angle. In he came again to think things over. Going outside was indeed a big step for this young owl and he was not going to be rushed. I pretended to work, not interfering, to let him make up his own mind on whether to venture out on his own or not. But I was holding my breath, as his decision could mean something big in both our lives. Then, turning, he strode purposefully to the door, hopped onto the step, down to the path and up onto the lawn. This time I went to sit outside to watch what he did, talking reassuringly so that he would not take fright.

But I need not have worried, as Wolly was far too interested in all the new things around him. Slowly, nipping at blades of grass and beak-testing the plants,

he made his way to the pool, pausing to look up at the sky and to gaze around. There was no sound from the garden birds. They too were holding their breath to see what he would do, and with me nearby they dared not mob him. He reached the edge of the pool and stopped in astonishment as the basking goldfish saw him and crash-dived out of harm's way. Wolly bent, nudged the water with his beak, and took a drink, deftly spitting out the unpalatable stuff with a shake of his head. He was about to wander off when he caught sight of one of the bigger fish lurking under a lily pad. He bent to get a better look. The fish disappeared. Then he spotted another, but it too vanished when he moved. This game went on for a few minutes while I watched, shaking with silent laughter, because I had a good idea what was going to happen next. I kept still—this was something that he had to find out for himself. And he did. He took a flying leap to land on what he thought was a solid surface on the water, but the leaf promptly sank under his weight. With wildly beating wings and much splashing he managed to extricate himself and came running to me, shedding water at every step. He had had enough adventuring for one day, and I carried him back indoors to dry off and have a rest. (I have noticed that any form of nervous strain can tire birds very quickly, but a short nap will soon restore their energy.)

During the summer heat I had been using a small hand-spray to cool the air in the studio. Wolly loved this and wanted to be squirted too. I thought that if he enjoyed it so much, why not try a bigger spray outside? That evening I got the garden hose, and adjusting the nozzle to a fine spray, started to water the plants around the pool and give everything a good wetting. As soon as Wolly heard the water pattering he came charging out of the door straight into the sparkling cascade, holding out his wings to get maximum benefit from the artificial rain.

As the days passed and his confidence grew, his exploration of the garden went further. Now he took short flights instead of walking, and found that it was much cooler to spend the heat of the day outside in the tree by the pool than it was sitting on top of the door. But as he was not yet six months old, I did not think that he was ready to cope with being outside at night, when he would have to meet and face, perhaps in a fight, the wild owls. All I had to do to get him back again was turn on the hose, and exhausted after the excitement of playing under the water, he would come in of his own accord to dry off and settle down for a deep sleep before dusk. All this was an excellent preparation for his eventual journey to the wild. On dull days he preferred to stay in and sleep, but now he could come and go as he pleased, and often he would grub around outside, catching snails, worms and beetles which would be brought indoors, and I would find these reposing on the carpet, or rather, what was left after he had finished tasting them.

By the end of that summer, Wolly had cast all his juvenile feathers, and shed along with them were many of his baby ways. He no longer lay down on his side, but slept with one foot drawn up into his feathers. Nor did he play so much. Now clad in sleek plumage of mahogany and cream, he stood fifteen inches from the crown of his magnificent head to the tip of his tail, with a wingspan three feet across.

2

Wolly finds a mate

The days now settled down into a routine that had not been possible with a baby owl around. Perhaps routine sounds rather dull—mine seems to be perpetually broken by the unexpected, which does liven things up a bit to say the least. If I've learned one thing in this life, it is never to say 'such and such can't happen' because it can, and does—frequently!

The day usually began with tidying the studio, then while Wolly had a rest from my exertions, I would leave him to sleep while I did the breakfast washing up and household chores. At eleven o'clock I would return to the studio to start my own work, and all should have been peaceful until mid-afternoon, when Wolly would wake and we would spend an hour or so playing together, after which I could resume work until six o'clock when it was time for me to go into the house and prepare our evening meal.

One of those unexpected breaks in routine happened once while I was working and Wolly was asleep. I was standing at the table with my back to the door concentrating on some drawings when suddenly, and without warning, Wolly flew down right on top of them, chittering with annoyance. Startled, I stepped back, tripped over something, fell backwards and sat down hard on the floor. Amid shrieks from Wolly and loud squeals, I found myself clutching a small piglet! Outside four more were watching the proceedings with great interest. Holding onto the piglet, I heaved myself up. The others 'woofed' and shot off down the path back the way they had come.

My first thought was, where is the sow? If someone had left our gate open she would be in the garden. Hurrying out, I caught up with the rest who were busy trying to squeeze back out under the garage gates. The sow was rooting in the drove oblivious of her errant offspring. She went on with what she was doing until she saw that I was still carrying the piglet, which was squealing loudly. So we formed a procession back to the farm; me in the lead with the protesting piglet, mother pig trotting along next, anxiously followed by a helter-skelter as the rest, not wanting to be left behind, pushed and shoved each other. On the way back after shutting them in the farmyard I discovered how they had got out. The field gate by the rickyard was lying flat on the ground, hooked off its hinges by the tremendously strong snout of the sow. I tried to lift the gate but found it far too heavy, so back to the farm for help. It took two of us to get it onto its hinges again.

'Er's a blasted ol' faggot. That's the third time the old girl has had thick-yer gate down,' said farmer Jim.

Living in the country one soon learns to fortify one's garden as much as possible against wandering animals but even 'the best laid hedge . . . gangs aft a-gley', and this was not the first time pigs had entered our lives. On another occasion, just as we were on our way out to dinner with friends, we saw with horror two pigs, as big as perambulating bathtubs, rooting in the middle of the lawn. John snatched up the kitchen broom and charged at them and I followed holding up my long evening skirt. Over the lawn, down the path, straight across the vegetable beds they ran, back to the hole they'd made in the hedge. With John bearing down on them, they both tried to get through at once, which gave him time to give the nearest a wallop across her bottom with the broom handle. It didn't hurt the pig, but broke the broom, which I still have, its handle now neatly spliced with string. (Typical local comment: 'Aah, I got an old broom too, had him for twenty years or more. Mind you, he's had several new handles and heads on him in that time.' Oh well, as they say in Dorset, 'If it's not one thing or the other—it's that, or something else' which seems a very good way of describing our 'peaceful' country existence. I might also add that in Dorset everything is referred to as 'he', except the bull, and that's 'she', which can be confusing at times. But one does get used to remarks like the one directed at a bulging, pregnant cat: 'I see he's going to 'ave babbies soon.')

For years we had been hearing from local people that whereas formerly there had been lots of owls calling at night, now they were hardly ever heard. Pesticides, the destruction of hedgerows and the clearing of trees probably caused the decline in their numbers, but we were lucky enough still to have a pair of tawnies nearby.

As the days drew in Wolly was learning to hoot. Already he would be up at the open ventilator window at night, hurling abuse and offensive shrieks at any of the local owls who happened to come near. It apparently took a lot of practice to achieve a proper hoot. This call of the tawny is not inherent, it is a copied call, and if a young male does not hear it first he will never make it on his own. Wolly took this business very seriously.

First he would take a deep breath, then closing his eyes and puffing out his throat, he would let go. At first the results were like a rusty steam whistle, uncoordinated rasping and wheezing noises. He would shake his head in annoyance, take another deep breath and start again. Gradually he got the hang of it, and one evening about a week later I was treated to the powerful triple challenge hoot of the male tawny—right in my ear!

Then he tried it out on the local owls, and soon it had a devastating effect. A wild pair claimed our garden as part of their hunting territory, and promptly turned up to see who this intruder on their patch might be. But to Wolly, the garden and all he could see of the fields around was his. The wild ones moved closer. Wolly, with feathers bristling, told them to clear off. Then the male came to the eucalyptus tree right outside the studio, and told him in no uncertain terms to go. When he didn't, the owl attacked the window. That was when I had to intervene and close the curtains. Wolly, though full-grown, was no match yet for an angry wild owl, and I feared for his safety.

Some nights I would wait with him for the wild owls to turn up. Wolly would be really enjoying himself, and usually started things off with a loud challenge. He would then hide at one side of the big window behind the edge of the curtain while I waited at the other. When the wild owl came close we would both jump out together. Surprised it might have been, but that didn't prevent it from coming back a few moments later. It was wonderful to see the two owls face to face, wings spread in mirror image on the window sill with only the thickness of the glass between them, but I was glad that the plate-glass was strong enough to withstand these encounters, for today it still bears the scratchmarks of

their talons. One night as I came out to the studio after dark, a wild owl flew low and fast around the corner and banged right into me. It clung to me for a second then shot away to the trees. I dare say it was not quite as startled as I was, because I was a familiar figure to them by then, but it had been flying too fast to look where it was going. These attacks went on intermittently all winter, ceasing as suddenly as they had begun, in mid-January, with no harm done on either side but the expenditure of much furious temper.

When dusk gradually got later and the curlews arrived back to nest by the river, Wolly showed even more affection toward me, and as spring came he would spend hours by my side, or at the open window with the breeze ruffling his feathers, gazing out into the distance with eyes half closed. I knew then what was going on in that intelligent little mind. The great outdoors was calling him.

His nights were spent in flying, as though he were deliberately training himself. Round and round, back and forth he would fly, with the draught from his wings making the air cold around. But still he didn't leave.

Then one morning just as dawn was breaking, I heard the sound I had been hoping for. Outside in the tree was a female. The two talked for a long time together, quietly and gently. The next morning the female was back again. Wolly was falling in love; and now he became restless. Well, he was ready. He had learned to catch his own food; he was fit and strong. A mate had come for him and she would be able to teach him all the ways of the wild that he needed to know. It was time for him to go.

The next morning at dawn I opened wide the garden door. Wolly came to my shoulder, gave a quick nuzzle to my ear with his beak—and was gone. I felt the powerful thrustback of his feet as he took off, but I couldn't watch him fly away.

Later in the morning, the blackbirds, with their chinking alarm calls, soon found where he had gone to roost. It was not far away, low down in the thick ivy round one of the elms that stood just beyond the garden hedge. I could do no work that day, but pottered around the place missing him dreadfully.

Dusk found me waiting by the hedge, and just before dark he flew up to a bare branch and called to me. We talked together until his mate came winging over the trees to join him, and later I watched him fly with her. Fast and true, strongly he went, and part of me too went with them into that star-covered night.

For the next seven days Wolly was back in the elm by dawn, and each evening I would wait for him to wake, and we talked together before he flew off. I think that one of the happiest moments of my life came at the end of that week. As I went to sleep I could hear him shouting his joy and freedom from the top of the trees, and when I woke at dawn I heard him call again before he went to roost.

On the seventh night he spent longer than usual with me, and I knew that he was saying goodbye. Gladly I told him to be gone and to prosper in his ways. I watched him go, flying swiftly and silently across the darkening fields.

3

Second brood

Oh, how I hated that empty studio now!

I collected up all Wolly's playthings: the velvet mice with string tails that I'd made him, his bits of beak-sharpening wood, and all the clutter that he used to hide up on his shelf. I thought of all the past months when I had only to look up to see him sleeping near me. Of the nights we'd spent together when I'd slept on the couch, and how he would haul me out from under the blankets by the hair to play with him at four o'clock in the morning! Of his constant companionship, and all that he had taught me, and how he had shared his life so completely with mine. And I hated to see the place looking so tidy in the mornings.

After a few days, I couldn't stand it any more. Life without an owl around just wasn't the same. Then the thought struck me. What had been done so successfully once could be done again. I picked up the phone and rang my friend in London to ask if by any chance he had heard of another orphan owl being found that spring. He hadn't, but suggested that a zoo might be the answer, as they often had young birds and animals brought to them that they didn't really want. Anyway, he said, he would make some enquiries and ring me back if he found one.

Days passed, and every time the phone rang I hoped it would be news for me. I'd almost given up hope when the call came. Yes, an orphan tawny chick had been found and sent to him, would I come and collect it?

The following morning I took an early train to town. But when the eagerly awaited box was opened we found not one owl, but two—and tiny things they were, barely two weeks old. They were so small that their dark blue eyes could not yet focus properly. When I was told that the smaller of the two had his beak clamped shut in fear and would take no food, I wondered how these little creatures had survived this far.

As soon as I got home, I took the two chicks from their box and put them in the warm, comforting darkness under my pullover where they snuggled up against me and slept. While I held them John cut up a meal, and when it was ready I clucked softly to them. At once they stirred and started to call for food. We put them in a cardboard box lid on some soft tissues, and as soon as I called again both beaks opened wide. From that moment on there was no more fear and they ate their fill, subsiding into sleep again when their little tummies were bulging.

It was the first time I had been able to get a good look at them. Shapeless little bundles of incredibly soft greyish down, all eyes and beak they seemed. On their stubby wings the feathers were just showing like an edging of scalloped brown lace, and the same on their tails. Their already strong legs were covered in fur-like down and the facial disks, not yet formed, were outlined with white that almost glowed when seen in a dim light. They woke briefly during the evening for another meal, but were fast asleep, flat out, side by side like a pair of kippers when I carried their box up to my room. Placing

it on a chair in the corner by my bed, I wedged it against the wall so that they could not fall out. Exhausted by their long journey, not a sound did they make all night.

At four the next morning I was woken by a soft cheeping, and when I opened my eyes, both owlets were standing by my pillow telling me that they were cold. So I just lifted the covers and the two spotlessly clean little creatures solemnly trundled in beside me, laid their heads on my arm, and we all went back to sleep again.

When John brought me a cup of tea at eight o'clock, he shook me awake.

'I can't find the babies,' he said anxiously. 'Where can they have got to? I've looked everywhere.'

I lifted the blanket to show him. He hadn't realized that the duties of a foster-mother included brooding her young!

The next day, with their eyesight improving, the youngsters started taking an interest in their surroundings and wanted to explore the living room, so it was time for them to be taken out to the studio. This meant that I had to sleep out there as well, because for the first two weeks, promptly at four a.m. they made the long climb from their box on the floor up onto the bed and waited patiently by my pillow to be taken into the warmth under the blanket.

For the first three weeks I fed them three times a day, starting at eight o'clock in the morning. From the very beginning they adapted to being fed during the day, going right through the night without making a sound. At first they slept in their little 'nest-box', but as they grew I made a bar-perch on a stand where they could roost side by side. At the end of four weeks I cut out the midday meal, as by that time they had doubled their size and did not need to be brooded any more. I wanted to make sure that the food they had would be as near to their natural food as possible, and that meant that I was faced with the 'ugh-job' of having to cut up mice for them! The multi-vitamins were replaced by Vitamins C and D and calcium each day to build strong bones and feathers, as faulty feeding at this age can produce rickets. They also had fresh beef with plenty of roughage (chicken feathers and fur wrapped round the meat). The amount that these little birds could pack away at one go was staggering.

At four weeks old, the bigger of the two, a female, took her first flight on sturdy wings. We called her Squeaky . . . because she never stopped! The younger,

a male, we called Chippy because he used his sharp beak like a chisel on anything he could get hold of. He launched himself into space a few days later and sat proudly, but wobbling a bit, on the back of my chair. Within a week, both had made it up to Wolly's high shelf, and spent most of their day sleeping with their little woolly heads poking over the edge. It was then that they took their first bath, splashing happily in Wolly's old drinking bowl. After they had bathed and preened themselves I grabbed the fast-moving Squeaky and parked her in the sun, spreading her wings out. Directly the warmth penetrated her feathers she thought it a good idea too, and Chippy, watching, immediately came and squatted by her side. If I were able to get Squeaky to do what I wanted, he would soon copy of his own accord.

Like Wolly the pair grew amazingly fast, and soon were very active instead of sleeping in the mornings. As they usually played on the floor, I had to put a notice on the door warning people not to come in, in case their sudden entry might frighten or injure the little birds. Squeaky grew very big and began to boss her younger brother about unmercifully. She wanted the best places on perches and window sills. She wanted to be fed first, and played with, knocking him to the ground in temper if she couldn't get her own way; she even flew at me once or twice. All would be peaceful, if not exactly comfortable for me as I tried to work with one of them on each shoulder. Then one would decide to climb to the top of my head. Of course the other, not to be outdone, would do the same thing. If I wasn't quick enough to remove them before they met at the top . . . well, I leave the rest to the imagination. But I got the distinct feeling that I would have been a lot safer roosting

at the top of the nearest tall tree. Oh for a pair of wings!

Squeaky couldn't resist the fascination of the pool in the garden and watched spellbound while I fed the goldfish. I was giving them FOOD, and she wasn't being included. One night, in the middle of the floor, and very dead, was one of the best and biggest comet-tails. Squeaky was sitting nearby wearing a look that plainly said, 'So that's what all the fuss is about. Don't think much of it, it tastes like cotton wool.' And she was speaking from experience. But she kept on trying, and I had to extract one soaky-wet owl from the pool more than once before she did too much damage.

The only time that the owls rushed for cover fast, was when a big heron flapped past the windows. He too was interested in the goldfish, but because the sides of the pool sloped too much for his liking, he didn't bother

with it and flew lazily off to raid the doctor's fishpond beyond the trees at the back of the cottage. That summer, a pair of herons would fly over the garden regularly every morning at four o'clock, and in a short time not one fish was left. They even ate the golden orfe.

I have found one thing that sharp beaks and claws can make little impression on, the old coat that I wear around the garden. It is warm and waterproof, with nylon fur collar and lining, the outside made of some sort of thick plastic material resembling green suede. But whatever . . . it doesn't tear nor can the fur be pulled out, although five owls and a cat have done their best to prove otherwise. Apart from keeping me warm, the old coat has many uses. Hung on the wall it is a soft perch for landing on and sliding down. Thrown on the couch it keeps baby owls occupied and out of mischief for a long time. It's a marvellous thing for hiding under and popping out suddenly to nip the feet of a playmate. The sleeves are soft tunnels that just ask to be explored. Only once did I have to put a stop to fun and games with it, and that was when one small chick entered a sleeve, only to come face to face with the other coming the opposite way. Greek met Greek, and neither would give an inch. There were furious squeaks and muffled shrieks as they disputed right of way, and I had to intervene and extract them—not an easy job, as they gripped the lining, spat and clacked, and turned their temper on me for spoiling the game. The coat may have been impervious to strong claws, but my hands were not.

Some of the things that birds and animals find for themselves to play with are quite odd. Someone gave me an Easter egg with a pink plastic orchid on top.

Chippy took the flower and for a long time it was his favourite possession until he lost it somewhere in the garden. When our cat was a tiny kitten, brought to us after being found starving under a hedge, I used an old toothbrush to untangle her matted fur, and long after she had grown up she would not be parted from it. One day when she was 'helping' me to pack some engraved crystal, she lost it. Luckily I decided to unseal the parcel and look inside. I don't know what the recipients would have thought if they had discovered that filthy old thing in with their glass where she had dropped it. Wolly had an old sable-hair paintbrush that he had stolen from me, a child's woolly mitten and a small plastic dog that he treasured.

* *

John came home late one evening and said that the car headlights had picked out an owl on the ground in the rickyard. We went up to see. It was still there and made no struggle as I picked it up and carried it home. When we examined it under the light, I was horrified to see its condition. It was painfully thin, filthy, and its beak long and overgrown. There appeared to be no sign of injury, but judging from its weak feet and unworn wing-feathers it had been in this state for some time. The bird was about a year old. Seeing no sign of disease I decided that it was safe to put him in the studio with the youngsters. This pathetically thin creature was weak with hunger and cried for food but was too far gone to accept any in his stomach for long. I cleaned him up and sponged his feathers and first thing in the morning called our veterinary surgeon.

Earlier we had seen a lot of dead rooks around . . . poisoned. It was a shocking sight to see these beautiful birds lying in the fields and now this tawny had picked up that lethal poison. There was just a faint hope that he might be saved, so he was given a slow-acting multi-vitamin injection to help him to get on his feet. At first, indeed he did recover a little. What food he took stayed down, he even slept with one foot drawn up, but he was far too weak to fly. From the first moment he was brought into the studio he showed absolutely no fear, in fact he seemed content only to have me near to stroke and talk to him. The fact that the two chicks were also there perhaps helped to reassure the poor little bird; but that was what made it all so heartbreaking, his perfect trust. He knowing that I was trying so hard to make him better, and I knowing there was practically no hope. When he wanted to move he would call to me, hop to my shoulder and use me as a carriage to the windows, where he would just sit quietly looking out. But gradually he became weaker. His food was rejected soon after being swallowed and he wouldn't leave my side. For five days and nights I never left him. The vet had been down again but there was nothing he could do. Then he came at once in answer to my call and there was only one more thing that we could do to save this brave little bird any more suffering. Sadly John and I buried him in the garden beside the trees where the owls call at night.

I shall never forget him.

It is not often that we need our vet, but when we do he comes swiftly to our aid. One morning when Squeaky and Chippy were four weeks old, they suddenly started to shiver and began falling about as though hopelessly drunk. Something was very wrong and I rang the vet at once. He examined them with great care and concluded that they had been poisoned. The first thing that we checked was their meat. But it was always fresh beef, kept in the fridge. It wasn't that. Nor was the poison from the sterile feathers I used to wrap the food in. We searched around in case there was something that they might have picked up while playing on the floor, but could find nothing. It was not until I mentioned that they had both taken a bath earlier that he found the answer. Building work was going on further up the road and as a precaution the water must have been over-chlorinated when the main pipes were opened. After their bath they had dried off and preened themselves, and in so doing had taken in undiluted chemical off their feathers.

Fortunately the effects soon wore off, but I was advised to boil every drop of water that I used for them for at least half an hour, and then let it stand for a few hours more before using it. I kept this up until after the buildings were finished, and we had no more trouble. Of course, rain water would have been ideal, but there was a drought at the time and our rain butt was empty.

So, despite their various adventures, these little ones thrived and grew.

* *

Wolly and his mate had nested down by the river, and in mid-August when their young were fledged and calling from the trees at night, Squeaky decided to join them. She was fed and cared for along with the rest of the brood and was for a long time still close to the house at nights. But little Chippy refused to go with her, although he had every opportunity and the door was left open all the time.

Three days after Squeaky had left, someone called to see John, and as we walked to the gate with him on leaving we found his wife, who had waited by their car, very excited.

'You will never believe this, I'm so thrilled . . . I've just seen an owl fly right over the car!'

'Have you never seen one before?' I asked.

'Oh no, not that close, and I do adore owls.'

'Well you never know your luck,' I said, and hooted into the gathering dusk. At once Squeaky replied and flew to me, landing on a low branch a few feet away. I have never seen anyone's face light up quite like that woman's did right then, as she stood almost rooted to the ground, not daring to move and not quite believing her eyes. Wolly was not far away, and we could hear his youngsters moving among the trees nearby. For a few minutes we were surrounded by hoots, squeaks and baby calls, then they flew away. Without a word, and as though slightly stunned, the woman got back into her car and they drove away. For some, and I can endorse the feeling, happiness is owl-shaped.

As they grew, Wolly's youngsters often came to be near Chippy. One evening John called, 'Come and look, there's an owl on the bird bath on the lawn.'

'Two more in the eucalyptus,' I said. 'No, three. Chippy is there with them.'

We stayed watching from the living room windows, not wanting to frighten them away, and I hoped that their coming might persuade Chippy to join them. But later, after the others had gone, I found that he had returned to the studio and was waiting to be fed as usual.

I was doing the after-dinner washing up on August the thirtieth when suddenly, there was a loud *Kee-wick* from the garden. I'd know that voice anywhere. I rushed

CLAIRE ROME

outside. There in the apple tree was my Wolly. With his brood grown and beginning to fend for themselves he had come back to say that he had not forgotten. He seemed overjoyed to see me, and turning on the full repertoire of his 'talk' gave me everything but the challenge hoot. How I longed to go right up to him. It was all I could do to stay with half the lawn separating us, but he was wild now, and if he trusted me then he might also trust a stranger, with dire consequences to himself. There are moments in one's life that defy description, but I think that I almost grew wings right then, because I was certainly off the ground. Owls must have long memories because it is now five years since he left, and from time to time he still turns up to greet me.

That winter, unlike the previous one, there was no aggression at nights. Wolly and his mate had taken over this territory from the wild pair, who now nested further away; and although he was often near, Wolly never attacked the windows and the nights were peaceful. Was it because he assumed that in the spring after he left I would naturally have another brood?

4

Owl Facts

One of the things that fascinates me is why people should think that a creature with superb night-vision should be blind during the day, but it seems to be one of the most popular misconceptions about owls. I know one thing, if owls could read, in bright sunlight they would have no trouble reading small newsprint fifteen feet away. They are extremely long-sighted, and I have noticed that this holds good until something is just a foot away from them, then they rely on feel and touch. It must be most frustrating to spend time stalking a spider on the wall, then having it move away from you because at close range you can't tell within an inch where it is. That's why I am so often asked, 'Catch it for me . . . I've missed the darn thing twice.'

When greeting someone, the owl will use its second pair of eyelids; in the tawny, they are a beautiful, shining blue. They are drawn slowly across the eyes as the owl blinks deliberately. This second lid, or nictitating membrane, is often referred to as a sun-shield, but I have never seen it used against bright light. It is an extra protective cover for the eyes, and is mainly used when fighting or when passing food from one bird to another, and when feeding their young. The eye of the tawny is much bigger than the human eye and needs to be protected at all costs, because without them the owl could not survive. The outer eyelids are a pale, pearly blue, and partially feathered, because when the owl sleeps it draws the bottom lid upwards, not the top one down as we do when we sleep. We still have vestiges of this second eyelid, as do most creatures. It can be seen very clearly when half drawn over the eyes of a sick cat, as a milky white film that appears from the inner corner of the eyes. In little owls, *Athene noctua*, the membrane is bright fawn. It varies in colour for different species of owls, but all of them possess it.

The owl also has very big ears. Set asymmetrically on each side of the head, enormous vertical slits run almost from the top of the eyes, right round the face on either side to just above the jaw-line. This opening is hidden behind a ruff of stiff feathers round the facial disk. Owls seem to like having the feathers between their eyes gently stroked, but for a long time I was rather afraid of touching anywhere near their ears in case I were to inadvertently hurt this very sensitive area. But sometimes they like to have their ears 'scratched' and if the fingers are introduced from behind, the earflaps feel like the rims of our own ears, and a little gentle rubbing there seems to go down very well.

The eyes of the tawny are dark brown, with a soft, dark blue pupil, and this can be seen quite clearly in direct sunlight. Baby tawnies are born with milky-blue eyes, which at first are only capable of picking up movement. At about the end of the first week they begin to focus properly and the iris gradually turns brown.

People ask why the owl is an 'upright' and not a bird-shaped bird, but they are bird-shaped underneath the long waistcoat of feathers that hangs down before them, as a thick padding that hides their real shape whilst keeping them warm on cold nights.

A healthy owl always sleeps on one foot, and there is a very good reason for this if you happen to be an owl. Two cold feet on a frozen branch in winter leaves you no time to de-frost for quick action if your dinner comes by. But one foot always warm and supple under your feathers is guarantee of success—well, almost always—providing your dinner has not seen you first. Owls carry hardly any parasites in their feathers. (There's not much point in having a good scratch just as your prospective dinner comes tootling by on the ground below.)

Not even its breathing must betray the hunting owl, so as it inhales, the feathers are automatically drawn in slightly, and relaxed when it exhales; so to all outward appearances it does not breathe but is absolutely still. Only by looking carefully at the point on the lower back where the folded wings meet, can the slightest movement be detected.

Most people know that the owls and falcons cast a pellet some time after they have eaten, but are unaware that most other birds do also. Even robins and blackbirds do not digest seed husks and other roughage, but perhaps because the birds are so small and the pellets so tiny, it goes unnoticed. But with all the raptors this pellet is much larger: bones, fur and feathers are all cast away when the goodness has been extracted from them. (Bones from chicken neck look like small sponges after the bird's strong stomach acid has been at work.) This roughage also cleans the panel in hawks and falcons and the stomach in owls, and prevents them getting slimy, because prolonged lack of roughage would lead to osteomalacia and the bird would die.

I have noticed that with owls the making of the pellet is not a completely automatic process, its actual shaping has to be done by the bird itself by stretching and squeezing the stomach to mould the pellet into a shape capable of passing back up the throat again. Unlike the hawks and falcons, owls do not have a crop, their food goes straight into the stomach, as ours does. Birds of prey digest and eliminate fairly fast (in owls it takes about three hours), firstly because excess weight of food would hinder their flying ability, and secondly, because they have to be opportunists, feeding when prey is available and not just at times when they feel hungry. With a limited capacity there must be room for food as soon as it is killed. Owls do not touch carrion or stale food.

Sometimes I am asked 'Does he . . . ah! what do you do about hygiene?'

At night newspapers are spread under favourite perches and all I have to do in the morning is pick them up for burning on the bonfire, and unless, which rarely happens, Owl has miscalculated, there is no mark anywhere else. The tawny is very clean, unlike the barn owl, which has the habit of using its nest for casting pellets and ah! yes . . . as well.

Many seem amused that I should make toys for an owl, but these so-called toys serve several useful purposes, the main one being that they are planned for destruction. The fact that the felt and velvet objects that I make actually look like mice is purely coincidental. What is needed is something strong and well sewn, otherwise it gets destructed in about four minutes flat. Wolly preferred chunks of beef that he could tear at for his meals, but while he was doing this the feathers wrapped round them for vital roughage would be dis-

carded. In the end I was forced to cut the meat into smaller pieces and the roughage then had to be swallowed, but doing it this way he was left with nothing to tear at. One morning I had seen a wild owl biting at something on a tree branch. The branch was fairly low, so later I was able to climb up and see what it had been doing. I found a patch where the bark had been gnawed off and scrape marks from the beak were still there. This gave me the idea of fetching a piece of firewood from the woodpile to see if Wolly would do the same thing. He did, but what I had not foreseen was that underneath the bark were woodlice, earwigs and other unmentionables, which promptly fell to the floor and tried to take up residence in the studio. Not at all a good idea. Hence the invention of the toys—they at least did not contain unwanted tenants.

Chippy has become a proper hoarder, and everything I give him, as well as items he has taken for himself, is taken up to his shelf. Often when he wakes in mid-afternoon he will 'housekeep'. First he turns to stare at his things as though taking an inventory, then potters over to sort them out, ending up with the shelf tidy, and what hasn't been knocked overboard is in a neat pile in the corner. It sometimes happens that while John is out during the day he will be given a mouse caught the night before, and on return he puts it up onto the place where I put Chippy's food at dusk. Chippy wakes, collects the offering and takes it back to his shelf. We love to watch the next bit. The mouse is parked beside him while Chippy scrapes away the pile of toys. Then he takes the mouse and puts it right in the angle of the wall, carefully covering it up with his things. But being a well fed bird, by nightfall he sometimes forgets his buried treasure and has to be reminded of it. He knows exactly what 'mouse' means, and will at once crash-land up in the corner—bits of paper, toys and general 'scringe' fly in all directions as he digs it out again.

I read somewhere that 'owls do not need, nor do they have, a sense of smell', but I have observed that the tawny does have a sharp sense of smell. Could it be that not being carrion-eaters thay need to be able to tell if their food is fresh? And who is to say that a wild creature so superbly designed by nature for survival, lacks one of the senses? Being curious, I wanted to test this 'no smell' theory. Next time a mouse was given to us that Chippy could not possibly have known about (as he had not heard a trap being sprung), I rubbed my finger in its fur. Then going out to him when he was fast asleep, and keeping all mouse-thoughts out of my mind, I reached up and silently waved my finger in front of him. It took exactly two seconds for him to wake and show the excitement usual when there is a mouse near, looking around eagerly and talking about it, so I brought it out and gave it to him. Q.E.D. There is a word, Ma'kheru, from ancient Egyptian, which means, to keep one's word with honour. This, to me, is one of the important things in life, not only in relation to other people but to birds and animals as well. I never make a promise I can't keep. That is why my charges know that if I say yes, then their trust is justified, but when I say no, there is no arguing the matter. But all the same it doesn't stop them grumbling just to relieve their feelings.

Everyone knows that all owls 'knack their beaks' to produce a loud cracking noise when they are annoyed—so books tell us. But having seen Wolly's beak slightly open while he knacked at a passing crow made me wonder. Then one day while he was on my shoulder, I looked up just as he gave a loud clack of warning, and saw how it was done. The tongue fits into a groove in the roof of the beak and the sound is produced by suction when the tongue is drawn sharply downward. I can now make a passable 'clack' of my own, but having no groove in the roof of my mouth, can never hope to rival the barrage of clacks that he can make when something startles him. The usual way of expressing temper is with a loud chittering, but the tawny can also give out with a sound like the tinkling of tiny bells when annoyed. And owls can get in a temper. The bigger the owl, the more furious it can become. And rage from a full grown tawny is no laughing matter—not safe to be too near either. Twice I have seen them attack someone, but luckily both times I was near enough

to intervene before damage was done to either party.

We had someone staying with us whom both the cat and I mistrusted. Nothing you could put your finger on, just a feeling of unease whenever she came into the room. Wolly was about five months old at the time and this 'friend' had really fallen for him in a big way. She had even been allowed to help me feed him. One night, just as she was leaving, she asked if she could say goodbye to him. I went out to the studio to switch on the dim night-light, and it was a good thing that I did, for as she entered the door, silently and swiftly he flew at her head.

Thinking that they had just collided, I brushed him away, putting on the main light as I did so. But he veered off, and, circling, came back to the attack. This time there was no mistaking his intention. Straight at her face he came, with razor sharp talons held stiffly out in front. There was not even time to think, but I remember flinging myself forward and calling to her to cover her face with her hands, get out fast and shut the door. She was shaken but untouched. Wolly was less easy to calm down. Needless to say, she has not been asked here again, nor is anyone, apart from ourselves, allowed near the studio after dark. The risk of someone losing their eyesight is too great—quite apart from the fact that I don't want the owls upset!

Wolly was always gentle and never once has he or any other owl used any pressure on me. However, John soon learned not to 'hold hands', because once held, he had a job to extract himself from their excruciating grip. The owl's foot has three toes facing forward and one back, but the outer toe is reversible and can be pointed back also. Many think that because it spends all its life in and around trees, the owl is a perching bird, but in fact it is far from happy if forced to spend too much time gripping a branch with its feet. The natural standing position for an owl is with the feet flat, resting on their thick padded soles, with the claws off the surface of whatever it is standing on. When resting, the claws of the foot drawn up into the feathers are folded like a jack-knife, into a fist.

It is difficult to know just how to describe these feet of a bird of prey. Structurally they are feet, but they are used as hands too, and a falconer describes his hawk as having hands and fingers, not feet and toes. The undersides of these feety-hands of the tawny resemble pinkish-

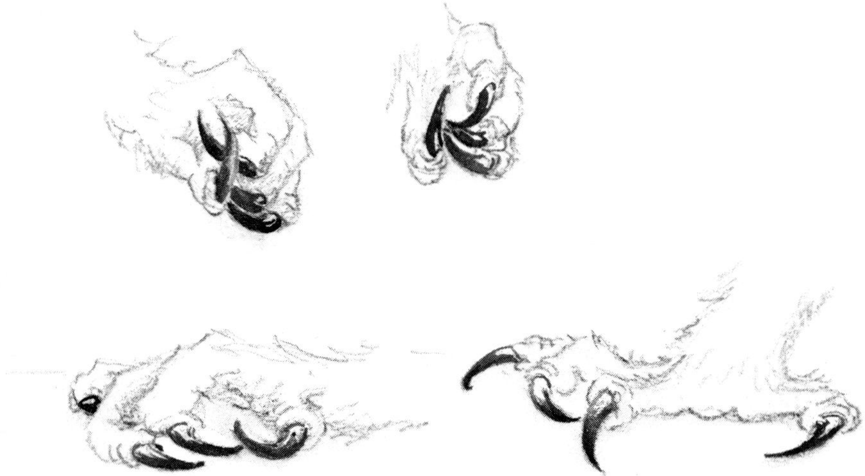

white sharkskin and are tipped with eight long, dark-brown, hooked claws, four to each foot. The main grip, as with the eagles, comes from the inner and back toes, like our first finger and thumb, the other two being used mainly for balance. But when caught in the vice-like grip of the tawny, I gather that one is by then far beyond the point of knowing what is gripped by which! People don't believe me when I tell them that the tawny is quite capable of crushing one's fingers—except the unlucky few who have been caught, and they don't need to be reminded. I have never used gloves when handling birds of prey, even eagles, as they are perfectly well aware of what they are doing, and know exactly how much they can hurt. I know this to be true because several times when an owl has landed on my bare shoulder, he has taken great care to keep those sharp claws lifted and use his wings for balance instead of gripping. Owls have even landed on my face when I have been lying down and not hurt me.

The barn owl has rather more curved, sickle-shaped claws than the tawny, the middle one of each foot being pectinated on the underside (like a small comb), to assist them with grooming and preening. Fishing owls have developed rough spicules on the soles of their feet to help hold the slippery fish which are their main diet.

Only once have I been scratched badly, and that was entirely my own fault. Wolly came winging through the dark one night to my shoulder just as I put my hand up. He altered course to the other side, and his claws, held forward for landing, brushed across my face. Their touch was so light that I thought nothing of it then, but when I came indoors I found that I was covered in blood from four great cuts that ran from forehead to chin. Only then did I realize just how razor-sharp those talons were. This happened the night before I was due to attend the opening of an exhibition of my paintings and I felt embarrassed at having to appear looking as though I'd been the victim of a gang war, but not one among the hundred or so people there that evening made comment on my odd appearance!

5

The most dangerous animal on earth

People coming here see what they think is a well-behaved pet snoozing on his perch. But these are no pets. Sleeping tigers can look attractive and gentle too! The bird they see by day is only functioning on a fraction of his owl-power. But as dusk falls a transformation takes place. Owl switches on. Alert, powerful, every nerve alive, he can be a scary individual to anyone who doesn't know him, the darkness making his flying shape even bigger, and a sudden shriek close up out of the silence can take some getting used to. No, the studio is no place for strangers at night, but I'm only another owl as far as these birds are concerned.

Despite books on birds in every bookshop; photographs, calendars, greeting-cards and endless things with owls on them, to the general public the owl is still the Barn Owl—white and ghostly. If he should choose to fly around the damp countryside at night when everyone else is tucked up in their nice warm beds . . . well, that's his affair. So to most day-time folk, Owl is still an unknown factor; strange, mysterious, eerie, with a touch of the supernatural about him. But there is nothing supernatural about owls, who are strong, tough characters. They have to be.

However, many myths still persist which help to foster in some minds the mistaken idea that there is something supernatural about owls. My dictionary defines supernatural as 'being beyond or exceeding the known powers of nature'. I like the definition as it goes on, 'the unseen, mysterious spiritual force or power that everywhere underlies and works in nature'.

I think the key lies in the word mysterious—something unknown and therefore to be feared. Maybe we could try to put this word into better perspective if we briefly examine, for example, the phenomenon of electricity. The modern world is practically run by it, and without it our daily lives would grind to a halt. We use it, but who can actually explain what it is? Yet people don't say 'I'm going to use the supernatural power', they simply switch on the light and take it for granted. We have become so used to electricity, it is not classed as something mysterious. Man can generate electricity and can control it to a certain degree, but how helpless he is when nature takes over and lightening strikes; and when it comes to harnessing the associated force, electromagnetism, he is even more at sea. The true north pole can be calibrated and is fixed to one spot, but nothing can be done to control the magnetic north pole which wanders about as the earth tilts on its axis. Our planet itself is one colossal, super-powerful generator, and everything, right down to the smallest atom and beyond, contains an electrical charge. Supernatural? Supernature is perhaps a better word to use. Something to be feared? No.

Birds use lines of unseen magnetic force on migration, and there are many ways that a dowser, or water diviner, can use them too. Bronze Age man, being closer to the earth, knew how to use and manipulate these forces, but as he became more 'civilized' and out of touch he lost the ability. Some people still have it, and I, being a dowser, am one of the lucky ones.

No one has yet explained satisfactorily how this dowsing works. When I am looking for underground water I pick up an electrical current. Is it caused by friction of water against soil or rock? The pendulum I use (a plastic bob at the end of a bit of string) is only an indicator like the dial on a machine, and has no power of its own, but it caused me great amusement once. I had been asked to locate some old wells, long since covered up and forgotten. Following a strong pull on the string, in a short while I managed to find them. One was in a stone-flagged yard behind a Regency house. I became worried because workmen were there and they had been carrying heavy scaffolding and timber right over it. The stone flags were worn thin and I had visions of someone falling through. My calculations made the well about three feet across, about thirty feet deep, and still full of water. Hurriedly I marked the place with a chalk ring and found the foreman to warn him to keep the men away from it. He was very interested, saying, 'I've never seen a dowser at work, how do you know when you've found water?' I demonstrated how the pendulum circled strongly when held over the well. Then he wanted to try his hand at it, and the men gathered round to watch. But nothing happened. I told him that if I touched him as he was holding the pendulum it should react. Reaching out, I touched the back of his hand with one finger. There was a loud crack as he got a shock; he jumped and fell sideways into a pile of timber. The shock he received was caused by static electricity building up in my body. The men all backed away from me, keeping a very respectful distance.

This same method of dowsing is used by the Japanese for sexing chicks. Adopting their method, I have found that it works not only when the pendulum is held over the bird, but even over a single feather. A mystery? Certainly, but nothing to be feared. There are normally only two methods of sexing baby owls, by X-ray or dissection, but I can add a third, which is painless for the birds and always right.

The origins of most myths are lost in the fog of time, and like the party game where 'send reinforcements we are going to advance' whispered from person to person, ends up as 'lend me three and fourpence we are going to a dance', most of these myths have been distorted and have lost their original meaning. However, one that does interest me is the connection between the goddess of wisdom, Minerva, and the owl. Owls abounded near Athens, hence Minerva (Athene) was given one for her symbol. The Greeks even had a saying, 'To send owls to Athens' meaning the same as our 'to carry coals to Newcastle.'

Also on the theme of wisdom, an old rhyme observes:

A wise old owl sat in an oak,
The more he saw the less he spoke.
The less he spoke the more he heard,
Why can't we all be like that wise old bird?

F.T. Elworthy wrote in 1895, 'It is unlucky to shoot an owl.' It certainly is in these more enlightened days. The owl is a protected bird, and the penalty is a heavy fine or imprisonment—quite apart from it being a cruel and utterly needless thing to do.

* *

Many people are startled to learn that there are one

hundred and thirty-two (maybe more) different kinds of owls. I say maybe, because surely somewhere in the deep forests there lives an owl family not yet caught, classified, dissected or even named. I like to think so anyway. They haven't caught the Loch Ness monster yet. Good for him! Many years ago Fennimore Cooper wrote the saga of the last of the Mohicans. That was it. Sad but true. No more Indians. But today, right now, there is a band of Mohicans, living quietly, minding their own business, but still there. So with owls. They go their own way and mind their own business, and in doing so are of tremendous benefit to man.

At this point I have to take issue with those who brand the owl as a cruel killer and talk about its 'cruel talons', referring to them as being the tools of its trade. Quite apart from the fact that the owl does not trade, it is not cruel. Yes, the owl is a killer: nature has made it that way. It kills to survive and to feed its young. It does its own butchering, but kills instantly, and not for sport. Nor does it play with its victim before dispatching it, or kill more than it needs. The owl is of immense help to man in the perpetual war against vermin—the rats which carry disease and destroy our food—mice, which do likewise—rabbits, which eat our crops—and some harmful insects. It is fashionable to criticize owls, but the same things are not said about the kestrels and hawks which take over when the owl goes to rest in the mornings, and which kill the same prey during the day. People would be horrified if one called the beautiful song-thrush a snail-basher, or referred to the garden blackbird as a worm-murderer, yet that is exactly what they are. To those who shudder and say, 'Oh, but owls eat meat' one can only ask, 'Did you enjoy your Sunday joint last week?'

No, we must keep a sense of proportion and remember that although there is plenty of sentiment in nature, there is no sentimentality, that is man's invention. None of the owl family has ever been proved harmful to man's interests—quite the reverse—but many unjust and wrongful myths about these birds are accepted without question. Many zoos now display a small cage labelled 'The most dangerous animal on earth'. Inside the cage is a mirror, and when they look in, people can see for themselves just who that dangerous creature is. And, I might add, the cruellest instruments known, are a pair of human hands, backed by a human brain. It is useful to remember the dictionary meaning of the word superstition . . . 'A false, misdirected belief based on ignorance'.

6

'Dial 0'

I have tried very hard, bearing in mind their future freedom, to keep the owls as wild as possible, but even they have to learn what 'No' means when I say it. I am *not* having the door open in the pouring rain just because a certain bird wants to sit on the step and catch the raindrops; nor will I have the back window open in a freezing east wind so that I work in a howling draught, however much *we* may want it; and: 'No, you can't have my best brush to chew up!' When they realize that 'No' definitely means no and not maybe, they put on an aggrieved expression that says, 'Oh well, no harm in asking, but if that's how you feel about it . . . .'

Our doctor's son Ian is a great friend of Chippy's, and one day when they were playing together he said, 'I wonder what Chip would do if I pretended to love that painting of the barn owl on the wall?' I had a pretty good idea what would happen, as Chippy had been watching with great interest while it was being painted, but as it didn't move he'd left it alone . . . so far. As soon as Ian made as though to stroke the bird, Chippy, with every feather bristling, gave a loud scream and flew at them both. Hastily I had to calm him down and turned the picture with its face to the wall, but it was a good few days before he would let Ian come near or have anything to do with him. Not only proof that the tawny can get very jealous, but in its way a fine compliment to my painting!

Wolly had also shown that he watched everything that went on. The year before, I had been commissioned to paint a large canvas of a deer park. During the work he found the top of the easel a fine vantage point from which to pass comments as it proceeded, and I was constantly having to request that he remove himself from the vicinity of the wet paint, to leave my brushes alone, not to fly off with the paint rag, and: 'How do you expect us to get this finished if you insist on sitting on my head?' At last, in spite of his help, the work was done and hung up to dry out. This was the first time that he had seen the completed thing from a distance. He examined it for a while, then before I could stop him took off to land, as he thought, in the large beech tree in the foreground. Bouncing off, he landed with a bump on the floor and turned to me with a look of bewildered surprise. Retreating to his shelf, he stared at the tree for a long time with puzzled interest, so the canvas was hurriedly lowered to the floor. After several minutes he tried the subtle approach. Landing by my chair he sidled up to the picture and cautiously tapped it with his beak, reaching up to touch the tree. Then he backed off to get a better view, bobbing about to examine it from all angles. I dared not laugh while this pantomime was going on for fear of hurting his feelings. He finally gave up in disgust and returned to his shelf, drew a foot up into his feathers and went to sleep.

The studio telephone is on the wall under that shelf, and has come in for a good bashing one way and another over the years. Owl asleep will suddenly wake to have a good shake, forget to grip hard enough with his claws and fall down, knocking the receiver off its hook; or while playing, miss his footing, with the same result. But Chippy will now deliberately knock the receiver to the floor because he has discovered that it makes a most interesting noise as it lies there. Many times when we are unable to get the dialling tone in the house, it's a case of 'I wonder if the owl has been using the phone?'—and sure enough he has!

The bell on the studio phone has been geared down so that we are not startled by its sudden loud ringing, but one day it ground to a strangled halt and I called the Post Office engineer.

'I can't quite make this out—the dial seems to be filled with a white deposit at the back.' He took the instrument to bits to clean it. As he scraped away, he said, 'It looks like chalk. How on earth did that get there?'

I laughed. Owl-in-residence stared hard at the ceiling, wanting no part of the blame, so I had to explain: 'Carelessness on the part of you-know-who,' I told him, pointing up, 'I cleaned it as best I could, but that's the reason we keep a cloth draped over it now.'

It only happened once, but it was a direct hit—and from an owl . . .!

* *

Part of the joy of having owls around is to watch people's reaction to them. Most have never seen one up close before, but automatically assume that an artist will have a stuffed model or two lying around to work from. Usually the visitor enters, glances briefly at Owl, who

is sitting motionless on top of the bookcase, staring out of the window. No reaction. A little later they idly look again. Owl, still unmoving, is now staring at the wall. The visitor looks longer this time and gets a slightly puzzled expression. I pretend that I don't know what's going on. After a minute, Visitor checks again, and now sees the bird looking out of the window as before. A bewildered did-I-really-see-what-I-thought-I-saw expression can be observed. Then while we are busy talking, Owl flies silently up to his shelf and the next time a glance is sneaked toward him—he has gone! This routine never fails to make my day. Once it completely unnerved a rather tough New Yorker who while talking leant against the wall right next to where Wolly was sitting. He received a sharp nip on the ear as Wolly came unstuffed in a hurry and flew noisily over his head.

This game doesn't work quite so well with Chippy, as he likes to be the centre of attention and gets quite annoyed if people neglect to greet him on entering—reminding them of their lack of manners with a low hoot. But even this can be funny, as sometimes those thus greeted can't make out where the noise is coming from, and don't think of looking up toward the ceiling. One couple even looked under the table. I asked what they were looking for.

'I thought I heard something in here—what was it?' said one.

'Don't worry, it's only an owl.'

'Oh' was the reply, as though it were an everyday occurrence. But all the same, although nothing further was said, there was a question mark left hanging on the air as they departed.

I was asked one day why Chippy was blinking, and explained that he did it in greeting and that the correct way to return his salutation was to blink slowly back. I was rewarded by the sight of three elderly, well dressed women standing in a row, all blinking and bowing solemnly at an owl.

What is it about an empty cardboard box that is so fascinating? Leave one around and soon one is sure to find a cat curled up inside or a puppy playing in it. A man and his wife arrived one day bringing a broken wooden figurine they wanted me to repair. After unpacking it they left the empty box on the studio couch and were standing talking and looking out at the garden, when suddenly, out of the corner of my eye, I saw Chippy glide silently down and disappear inside the box. As they were about to leave the woman said, 'You won't want to be cluttered up with this, I'll bring it back when we collect the carving' and reached out to close the lid.

'Be careful!' I exclaimed, putting out a hand, 'There's an owl inside.'

Slowly, and with faces completely blank, they turned to stare at me.

'I know what you're thinking', I told her, 'but very gently lift the flap and look.'

She did—to be met by a pair of indignant dark eyes as Chippy glared at her for spoiling his cosy retreat.

These days, more than before, people seem to have become geared to the place in which they live. Up on the hills not far from here, surrounded by beautiful forest land, the thoughtful council have made a large, fenced enclosure labelled 'Picnic Area', where because the ground is hard enough all year round, cars will not become bogged and plenty of litter bins are provided. But with glorious country walks and views all around, we have noticed that visitors to this part of the world

are reluctant to leave their cars. There they sit, eating their lunch, listening to their radios and reading newspapers and never venturing outside the gate. Then, having 'enjoyed the country', off they go again.

Once while I was busy with a client in the studio, John went out to a woman who was waiting by their car; she was muttering to herself and banging her fist on the gate. As he approached she said, 'You must be raving mad to live in a place like this. Look at it. There aren't any houses! There aren't any people! Where are the shops?'

John, a bit nettled, said, 'We've got a very good shop in the village, and our nearest town is only three miles away. Besides, we like it here.'

But she didn't want to know, and still talking to herself, got back inside her car and slammed the door. Agoraphobia must be a terrible thing to have to live with.

In contrast to the 'owl in a box' episode, where the couple's reactions on seeing Chippy were complete astonishment and disbelief, was the reaction of a countryman who came to the studio. He was a big man who spoke quietly and moved softly. This stranger stood just in front of the door with his back turned to Chippy, who was on top having a snooze. After talking for some time, he mentioned what a nice quiet place I had here to work in. I asked if he had seen the owl. 'Oh yes,' he replied. 'About a year old isn't he?' I had not even seen him look at Chippy, but he had, and instantly accepted his being here as the most natural thing.

7

'Dirty great chicken'

The grass in the field next to the house stood tall and ready for cutting, the sun giving promise of hot days to come, and ideal haymaking weather. All the windows were wide open to catch as much of the passing breeze as possible, so I was not too surprised when I went back to the studio after doing the breakfast washing up, to find Chippy gone. Calling, 'Now where have you got to?' I began to tidy the room. Hearing me, he came back fast, straight to my shoulder, very excited about something. 'What have you seen?' I asked, because when I looked outside, the field seemed empty to me, the only movement was the grass rippling in the golden light. But Chippy was staring hard at a spot about half-way across the field, so I went out to have a look. There was something there all right, and from the distance it looked like the tail of a fox, half hidden in the grass. As I went over, a big collie dog got to its feet and went slowly away through the far hedge. I had not seen it before, but knowing that several newcomers had recently moved into the village I presumed that it too had just arrived, and thought no more about it.

Later that afternoon there was more excitement from Chippy. He was flying back and forth, which was unusual for that time of day, when normally he is sleeping. When I looked outside, the dog had come back and was curled up by the gate only three yards away from us. This time it did not go away when I went out, but stood up, looking at me with eyes filled with sadness. Opening the gate, I called and the dog came slowly, with head hanging and tail drooping. Behind me I heard the sudden flurry of wings as Chippy flew to the safety of his shelf.

The dog followed obediently as I coaxed her along the path and into the house. I knelt down beside her. 'Oh poor Lassie. You are lost, aren't you?' At the name her head came up and she put her long muzzle trustingly in my hands. She was a lovely dog, in beautiful condition, her long coat silky and well brushed . . . a well cared for dog. Now she panted a little so I offered a dish of milk which she accepted delicately, like the true aristocrat that she was, and while she was drinking I rang the police. 'Oh bless your heart,' said a country voice, 'we've been looking all over for that dog. She's been missing since yesterday. You hang on to her m'dear, we'll tell the owner and put him out of his misery.' And they did, quickly, because shortly afterwards a van came down the lane. That was one reunion I wouldn't have missed.

Apparently, the previous day the farmer had taken her for a walk down by the river after milking time, someone on the other bank had fired a shotgun and the terrified dog had run off. Her owner had called and called and searched until after dark, then had spent a sleepless night worrying that she might try to get home to the next village along the main road, which carries a lot of heavy traffic. All through the night he had imagined her lying injured, or worse, by the road. But she had more sense. She had come up across the fields away from the river and was waiting to be found.

'I do thank you sincerely for finding my Lassie' he said, after they were reunited.

'But it wasn't me, it was my studio assistant who did that. Come along and meet him.'

That was something else I wouldn't have missed. Well, it's not every day that a lost dog is found by a tawny owl, though to judge from Chippy's smug, self-satisfied expression, it could well have been.

* *

To keep Chippy supplied with fresh food we trap field mice, and sometimes voles, but owls will not touch shrews unless driven by hunger, as they contain a certain bitter element that makes the smell and taste offensive to both owl and cat. (If forced to eat a shrew, the owl will only take the head and front part, leaving the rest.)

For some time, each morning our mousetraps in the garden had been sprung but there were no mice, and Chippy was forced to dine on sliced beef from the freezer. Sometimes only a head was left in the trap, the rest having been eaten by something. I was very puzzled over this, as our 'trap forts' were made with great care so that the holes left are too small for birds to get in after the cheese, and the stone blocks surrounding the traps too heavy to be moved by cats, foxes or badgers.

I had on several occasions been called from the house by a shriek of indignation from Chippy to find a farm cat trotting off with his mouse, plus mousetrap. Chippy knew that the trap was his, but he was not going to risk taking after the cat to get the mouse back. I had to chain the traps to the ground and surround each with a fortress of bricks. Even then we continued to lose some of the mice we'd caught. No cat is strong enough to shift bricks, so perhaps it was a badger or fox. Replacing the bricks with stone blocks seemed to deter most four-footed marauders for a while.

Yet, once again, something was getting in to take our mice. Then one afternoon, Chippy, quivering with excitement, flew to the side window. At first I couldn't see what he was looking at, but I knew from experience that he notices the slightest movement, and it took me some time. Then I saw it. Snaking through the grass came our trap raider . . . a weasel. Quietly I opened wide the window, and Owl and I leaned over to watch as it came up the bank and into the garden. As it came right under the window I nudged Chippy. 'Go on. Go get him. Quick. He's going straight for your mice.' But with the sun shining brightly, the well fed tawny decided suddenly that he wasn't going to risk going outside, and

flew back to his roosting place, and ignoring my indignant remarks went to sleep.

That presented me with a problem. The loss of our mice was serious, because while fresh beef is full of nourishment, I wanted to keep his diet as near as I could to that of an owl living in normal conditions in the wild. But how to catch the raider?

After much thought, I bought a cage rat-trap, the kind which catches the animal without injuring it. (It is so arranged that as the bait is approached, the weight of the rat tips it into an inner chamber from which it can't escape.) I baited it with bits of fresh beef and in a short time had not one, but a pair of weasels. We took them to rough ground a long way from here and released them. And the next morning Chippy had a big fat mouse for breakfast.

But Chippy isn't always so coy about going out of doors in the daytime, and one day was sitting on my shoulder while I was doing a bit of weeding around the fish pool. Suddenly he gave a loud *clack* and flew back indoors just as the postman came round the corner of the house.

'I wouldn't let a dirty great chicken sit on my shoulder,' was his greeting.

Chicken? Then I realized that to someone who didn't know what it was, the quick glimpse of a large brown bird could mean only one thing in the country.

'A chicken . . . . Do you *mind*,' I said. 'Come in and meet the flying fowl!'

The postman, new to this round, stood entranced, hardly believing his eyes. But he does now. He has had to deliver several letters addressed to 'Master Chippy Rome', usually cards with owls on them from Chippy's admirers. These are much appreciated and end up the

way most of his toys do ... chewed to confetti and strewn all over the floor.

* *

I had been doing some work for a film company who occasionally come to me when they need the help of an artist. This time the director had been here every day working with me, and we had been re-touching enlarged photographs ready for re-filming. Chippy had cheerfully put up with the disruption. A compressor had been chugging away for the airograph machine, intermittant clouds of smoke rose from the director's pipe, and the floor was littered with tripods, projectors, boxes, reels of film and other paraphernalia. He could have gone for a quiet snooze outside but was far too interested in watching what was going on. I enjoyed the work but it was a bit of a strain, so when it was over the following afternoon I decided to have a couple of hours rest on the studio couch. It was a cool day so I pulled a rug over me and fell asleep. Some time later I awoke, so hot that my face was streaming with moisture, and when I opened my eyes it was dark. Half awake, I could not make out what had happened. Then as my eyes focussed I realized that it was not dark . . . there was light shining through feathers. No wonder I was hot! Chippy was sitting on the pillow by me with one wing spread protectively over my face.

Another time that wings were spread in protection around me was when I spent an afternoon at a show where large birds of prey from a falconry centre were on display. There were hawks, eagles, vultures and kites there, and I had asked permission to make drawings of them. As I found a corner in which to sit, the falconer warned me to beware of a big sea eagle which was on a long bar-perch nearby. 'He can be very vicious' he said, and looking at the huge hooked beak, I could well believe it. Gradually the eagle sidled along the bar until he was near me. I began to talk to him as I worked. The eagle moved closer and closer, until he was leaning up against my arm, and I could feel the warmth from his body. He spent over an hour contentedly watching what I was doing. This eagle, *Haliaeëtus albicilla*, is a very big bird, the largest of the European eagles. The female measures up to three foot in length and over eight foot across the wings, and at this very close range even the male gave one the impression of enormous size. When the time came for him to be taken away for a display flight, in a flash he spread his wings in front of me and defied the falconer to come any nearer. I had to move away before he would calm down.

All the usual noises that one gets from living close to a farm are soon taken for granted by the owls: chain saws, hedge cutters, even the baler and combine harvester are ignored after a while, but there is one thing that always reduces an owl to an elongated, slit-eyed shape fast, and that is the humble metal wheelbarrow. It's not the squeaking wheel, because I oiled it; it's just that the silly thing rattles and bumps along the ground. All the owls hate it. Chippy didn't care much for storms when he was young, and one night when crashing thunder was right overhead he was rigid with fear when I went out to him. We soon cured that. Making as much noise as I could I bounced around him, shouting at the thunder and yelling at the lightning, pretending it was all great fun. (It's a good thing no one was near to witness my near-lunatic performance.) But it worked, as in a few minutes Chippy joined me at the window and he too started hooting at the thunder and ended up thoroughly enjoying himself. It is not the noise that causes fear, it's the vibration. When one of the big elms in the field near the house had to be felled, it was close contact and a steady soothing voice that was needed, as the huge tree fell with a crash that shook the house. The tractor is ignored, but the owls do not like it when ploughing is going on. Nor do I. One can feel the earth shaking from a long way off. Our cat leaves the house in a hurry to avoid, not the hum of the washing machine, but the vibration of the spin-dryer. And the guns from Salisbury Plain or blasting from Portland will make the pheasants crow at night. But while we understand what causes things to go bump in the night, it still doesn't mean that we have to like them.

While owls can be aloof and distant with grown-ups, they show a different side of their characters with children, who are allowed to take liberties. Should any adult presume to touch any 'personal' thing belonging to the owls there is instant uproar; but I have seen a three-year-old child sitting happily on the floor with a full grown tawny bouncing round her, both intent on the game they were playing together. It is now the *in* thing for local children to come and 'see the owl' and bring mice caught for him, in paper bags. Now, anyone entering with, or rustling a bag that doesn't contain a mouse, soon hears all about it. The thought has just crossed my mind: Wolly to offspring, 'Keep a sharp lookout for paper bags when you hunt . . . that's where the best mice live. . . .'

Young babies are a special attraction. Owl gets a soft, gentle, and rather soppy expression on his face, and ignoring everyone else, concentrates all his attention exclusively on the infant. Do they, I wonder, react to the wide-eyed innocence and absence of fear in each other's gaze? I remember a rather fierce eleven stone bull-mastiff acting in the same way with very small children; and I am told that once at the age of two I was found sitting between the front feet of a huge shire horse which in those days delivered our coal, playing with the long 'feathers' on its legs. A horse so vicious, I'm told, that it had to be muzzled. Apparently it took half an hour and the combined efforts of my mother and the coalman to persuade Horse to part with his new playmate. Absence of fear will get you everywhere in the natural world of birds and animals, who can pick up bad intent in a flash. A clear demonstration of 'as you think . . . so you are', and 'if thou trusteth not . . . then thou most assuredly will not be trusted in return!'

8

Personalities—owl style

Grazing animals which herd together to search for food do not need a very high intelligence for survival (although they have a lot more than we give them credit for at times). Grass may have to be looked for, but it doesn't run away when you've found it. Creatures who hunt in a pack need craft and guile more than intelligence. Under the leadership of the fittest and strongest male a strong 'pecking-order' exists, especially with wolves, where everyone knows their right place and is kept in it. However, a nocturnal predator is a loner, it can't call for back-up support but has to think things out for itself and be wise to the ways and haunts of its intended prey, as they are equally well equipped for surviving in darkness. It's a case of 'them or me, and if they win . . . I go hungry.' The owl must be familiar with every inch of its chosen territory and use endless patience combined with surprise attack. All raptors, from the eagles down to the smallest owl (and the smallest is no bigger than a sparrow), have to be able to fight to claim and hold a hunting area for themselves, otherwise the food supply would soon run out. Owls mostly mate for life and will allow only the chosen female to share their feeding area in winter, although they do not come together until the mating season. Thus owls need quick intelligence, a strong sense of possession and a good memory.

The tawny is the only one of Britain's five indigenous owls which will make an all out attack on anyone going too near its nest, although the short-eared owl will swoop and dive over intruders to drive them away. Owls need to be quick witted, not only to catch their food, but in order never to put themselves in a compromising position or a tight corner where there is no wing space for a quick getaway.

The tawny never pushes things. It will spend a long time examining terrain, checking and re-checking, judging angle and distance and relative position of one thing to another, eliminating as far as possible the chance of getting caught. Its last line of defence if taken off guard on the ground is to throw itself on its back and present a set of claws at the ready, which only the very foolhardy would dare go near. Thus the owl is cautious, preferring to go its way in peace unless interfered with. The owl is an honourable bird, only showing hostility after provocation. But it does not, when associating with humans, fawn or ingratiate itself. Like all predators, winged or four-footed, it has innate dignity and a certain aloofness, plus exquisite good manners toward those it trusts. It's all or nothing with an owl, which will fight against interference in its life, but once it gives its loyalty, that loyalty is complete. It goes without saying that if anyone were to raise a hand against me in the presence of one of the tawnies here, they would instantly be in for a very hard time indeed!

There used to be a time when it was thought that all Orientals looked the same (and I dare say we all did to them too). Owls of the family *Strix aluco* may all look alike to most people, but this is far from the truth. Each tawny is an individual; he not only looks different from his brother but no two voices are the same, and each differs in character, just as no two humans are exact copies of each other.

Wolly was definitely lord of all he surveyed, with a striding, purposeful walk. Chippy has a comic bounce when he moves on foot, is much quieter, and asks for what he wants. Squeaky, huge, noisy, happy extrovert, just TOOK, bossing everyone, including me. But all have been highly intelligent, never needing to be told anything twice. They have had a great capacity for affection, a firm spirit of independence, a good healthy temper, and most important of all . . . their dignity has been kept intact.

Owls and cats are very alike in many ways. Some say that cats are creatures of habit, but I would say rather they are creatures of changing habit. They will pursue a course for just so long, and just as one gets used to it switch to something else. The tawny will roost for a while in one place then change to another. Perhaps instinct still works with the cat, as with the owl, impelling it never to stay long enough in one place to sleep in case a stronger predator gets a chance to creep up on it unawares. It may be that really tame domestic cats don't follow this inbuilt precaution but ours was born in a hedgerow, and while utterly trusting with us, was always wary of strangers.

Both cats and owls like to see everything in its accustomed place. Bring something new into their own special territory and there is no peace until it has been thoroughly inspected, tested and approved.

It is interesting to watch Chippy in the evenings when he wakes up. First he will look outside to see that all is

Chippy and Squeaky at 4 weeks old.

'Scratch my chest!'

Taking off.

'Watch me!'

Coming up to land.

Chippy.

'That's mine.'

Chippy on his shelf.

well, then the room gets a good going over. Even the studs on the walls have to be checked to make sure that no one has moved them, or that they themselves are not moving, and woe betide the poor benighted little spider or moth that is trying its best to imitate a spot on the wall—it doesn't stand a chance after Chippy has seen it. Recently men were busy cutting the hedge across the field from us, and all day chain saws had been at work. But noise in the distance is not cause to an owl, he is interested only in effect. When Chippy woke at dusk to see no hedge where there had been one in the morning, he was most indignant, and grumbled about it most of the evening. Not far from us there are three big elms due to be felled soon, and I can guess what he will have to say about that too!

Squeaky took to her freedom like a duck takes to water—although it was some time before she flew off for good—but little Chippy on his first outing was much more timid. From the studio windows the nearest tall trees were about a hundred yards away, and from that distance they did not look too big. He followed me out to the terrace by the pool, and while I stayed to reassure him he had a good look round. Going over to the eucalyptus tree and patting the lowest branch, I called him. After a little hesitation he came to my shoulder and from there hopped to the nearest branch. The breeze caught and ruffled his feathers. It was Nature's gentle hand calling one of her own creatures back to her, and he responded by going a bit higher. Encouraged this far he flew to a branch about twelve feet up, and from this new vantage point looked down with feathers roused in interest. Then he looked up. Overhead hung the great branches of the elm at the back of the house. The sight of them spread over him like moving tentacles

of some great octopus was too much. He simply had no idea how huge a tree could be when seen from right underneath. He fell off the branch in surprise, landing in a heap in the plants below. He forgot all about nature's gentle hand, and uttering a mournful little wail picked himself up and flew to my arms. After one more scared look up at the big tree, he shot back to the safety of the studio as fast as he could go.

It is amazing how many expressions a face covered in feathers can make. They range from the near-angelic to a perfect imitation of a thin tree branch with slanty slit-eyes. One thing a tawny does not do is get an evil look on his face, he leaves that to his yellow-eyed brethren, the eagle owls. Like the true falcon, he is a gentle-eyed bird. I usually know when trouble is in the offing by the secretive look that means, 'Just wait till you're not looking, that paper you're working on will tear beautifully when I get my claws into it!' I was watched with great fascination while putting some impact adhesive tape over heat cracks in a plasterboard wall. I was too busy to notice Chippy's expression or I should have known what was coming. A few minutes later there was a loud ripping sound and a great flapping of wings as, pulling and tugging, he backed off across the floor with one end of the tape in his beak. It took me five minutes to remove the sticky tape from his tail after that effort. But I must admit he was right—the tape does make a most delightful ripping noise when pulled off the wall!

A brave bird too is Owl. Once when out together for a quiet walk up the lane we met the vicar, late for Sunday school, hurrying along, cassock flapping and billowing round his legs. Owl on my hand drew himself up to full height, and let go a barrage of *clacks* that left nothing to the imagination. The louder the clacks became, the redder got the vicar's face, but Owl, holding his ground, did not fly off my hand—only at the very last moment adding further emphasis to his feelings by letting go all down my coat.

With inquisitive creatures like these it soon became second nature never to leave anything about that could harm them. Drawing pins, paper clips or nails are of no interest to an owl, and soft things like elastic bands, even if swallowed do no harm, as they are soon returned wrapped neatly around the next pellet. In my work I use a stripping knife a lot but would sooner put the shield on and off a hundred times a day than take the slightest risk of a small foot getting anywhere near its razor-edged blade—especially as the handle of the knife is red, an attractive colour to any predator. Nature's warning colour is yellow: think of wasps, hornets, bumblebees. Only man would think of using the colour of life, red, for danger. Owl is quick to pick out colours on the red end of the spectrum, and I suspect, ultra-violet, but has no use for the green end: blues, mauves. Why should he? He doesn't eat flowers. (Although here he enjoys tearing them to shreds from my vases.) And whoever saw a purple mouse anyway?

I have learned to close the turps jar and cover up paints when answering the phone, and not to leave pins or needles around, or my lunch, as sandwiches have to be examined to see if they contain meat. John made the mistake one day of bringing his ploughmans lunch to eat in the studio, but no sooner had he sat down than Chippy landed right in the middle of it. I had to clean them both up that time, as they were liberally plastered with gooey pickle that John had been all set to enjoy with his bread and cheese. In fact, those who say, 'Oh, doesn't he look sweet, sitting there on his shelf' can have

simply no idea how that innocent looking creature can swiftly turn into one big *pest bird*. Half the time I don't even have to turn my back for trouble to start, and anyway I enjoy a game as much as he does, and am just as much to blame.

The big beak that gets itself into everything will, like our fingernails, soon grow too long if it doesn't get constant wear. Food becomes impaled on the end of it and can't be swallowed. I make sure now that there are always beak-sharpening twigs around. When Wolly began his first adult moult in the spring before he left I gave him extra calcium to help grow strong feathers. That was fine, but his beak grew hard as iron because of it and became too long, so not knowing quite how to cope, I called the vet. Poor man, little did he know what he was in for.

Wolly resented being wrapped in a towel like a bundle of washing with only his head left sticking out. He resented being laid flat on a cushion on the table, and worst of all he resented being touched by a stranger. He struggled and swore, he clacked and twisted his head about, he wriggled like an eel and clawed the towel. The operation itself didn't hurt any more than it does to have one's nails cut, but his dignity suffered acutely!

9

Dropped feathers

Whatever I do, things always seem to come back full circle to the first owl I raised. This year he and his mate nested in the very tree at the end of the garden where he went to roost on the day he left here. It is as though he too is unable to break the ties that bind us together. Then in June a most wonderful thing happened. The evening was still and warm when just at dusk baby owls began to call, and I walked down the field to see if I could find them. Slowly, silently I went, barefoot over the grass. But I did not reach the elm, for suddenly they came to me, these young of my first protégé. Three there were, about two months old, and nearly as big as their parents. They flew and landed on a branch only just above my head. Sitting in a row, they leant over and mewed to me. When I spoke to them they answered, and we stayed together until it got too dark for me to see. As I walked back they followed through the trees, only flying away when I reached the garden. Although born free they showed absolutely no fear at all.

It is possible to have telepathic communication with all animals, but having such a rapport with owls, I find it easy to get onto their wavelength. Sometimes they will sing to me their rarely heard greeting-song, a beautiful one-note theme warbled in verses or stanzas. A verse is sung, and then the singer will pause, waiting for a reply before starting again; sometimes we keep up this duet for minutes on end. I am used to this now, but was not prepared for the same thing to happen from a strange owl of another generic family that I had never seen before.

We were at a Wildlife Park in Somerset and I had been telling the Curator about this special song of the tawnies. We were standing by a big aviary that housed a pair of magnificent eagle owls which were watching us, when one of them, the male I think, blew out the feathers of his throat. Very excitedly I said, 'Look, I do believe he is going to sing.' And sing he did. It was exactly the same but in a very deep voice. The owl was looking straight at me and treated us to about six verses. The Curator was astonished.

'We've had those birds for over six years, but I have never heard them do that before!' and looking closely at me he asked, 'Do you suppose that it has anything to do with your wearing glasses?'

No, of course not; but I knew that splendid bird must have picked up my thoughts. And in the same way Wolly's youngsters knew that they had nothing to fear from me.

Apart from the usual hoots, shrieks and other loud calls, the tawnies also have a repertoire of gentle and more intimate ones. Some are so quiet that they can only be heard from a few inches away, but it is a definite—if limited—language of phrases; and as I have proved, it is possible to understand and pass simple messages with it. When that fails, there's always that old telepathy, which works both ways.

In fact, it was a three way affair recently.

As I was starting work one morning, John put his head round the door saying, 'I'm just off to town, are you all right for Chippy's meat for tonight?' and knowing that there was enough in the fridge for one more feed I replied, 'Yes, we shan't need any till tomorrow.' But later as I worked I kept getting the thought, 'I'm hungry . . . I'm hungry.' Looking up at Chippy, I saw he was leaning over staring hard at me, and that was definitely where the message was coming from. He shouldn't have been hungry, as there had been nothing left at his feeding place that morning. Probably what had happened was that the night before, while he was eating, one of his pals had turned up, and going to the window sill clutching his meat he had dropped it outside. I can imagine how he must have felt when the wild owl swooped quickly down and stole his dinner from right under his beak! I cut up the rest of the beef for him and he ate the lot. Poor little chap, he had been hungry. I sat down to try and reach John with the thought, 'More meat . . . meat for Chippy,' until although I didn't know where he was, I felt he had picked up my message.

An hour later he came back and the first thing he said was, 'A most extraordinary thing happened. While I was out just now I kept hearing in my head, "Get meat for Chippy". It was very odd because for a while I couldn't think of anything else.'

'Well, and did you?'

'No,' he replied, 'I didn't because I remembered you saying that you had enough until tomorrow.'

Then I told him what had happened. Our telepathy had worked beautifully but it went wrong in the interpretation, and that cost him another trip to the butcher's shop that afternoon.

* *

The yearly moult usually starts at the end of March just before the owls are due to leave here, but until Chippy's moult I had not been able to follow it through to the end. Now I have. And I have come unstuck with my owl-project—because Chippy refuses to leave!

As spring approached last year he watched the garden birds with great interest. But it was difficult to know if it was their chasing and pairing that fascinated him, or whether he just looked on them as so many potential flying dinners. The windows were left open night and day but all he did was just sit there watching. I took him outside and tried launching him. At dawn and dusk I tried again. But it didn't work. Instead of flying away he took a wide circle round the garden and flew straight back into the studio. Then a female turned up, and my hopes rose. But even that was no use, and after a week of courting and soft-talking him she left in disgust to find another mate. In the words of a friend of ours: 'I think you've got a cissy-bird there.' But owls are like people, all different, and some are naturally more shy and home loving than others. Chippy is just not the bossy, outgoing type. Maybe he has not forgotten how hen-pecked he was by big sister Squeaky when they were small. Or as someone else said 'That bird really is wise—he knows when he's on to a good thing.' But whatever the reason, secretly I'm delighted that he is still here, although the choice of leaving is his at any time for the taking.

So last year was the first time that I was able to follow the moulting process right through to completion. This moulting is not just a haphazard shedding of feathers; even in this, nature has an ordered rhythm and sequence. Around the end of March it started with more frequent bathing and a lot of shaking and fidgeting. Then the

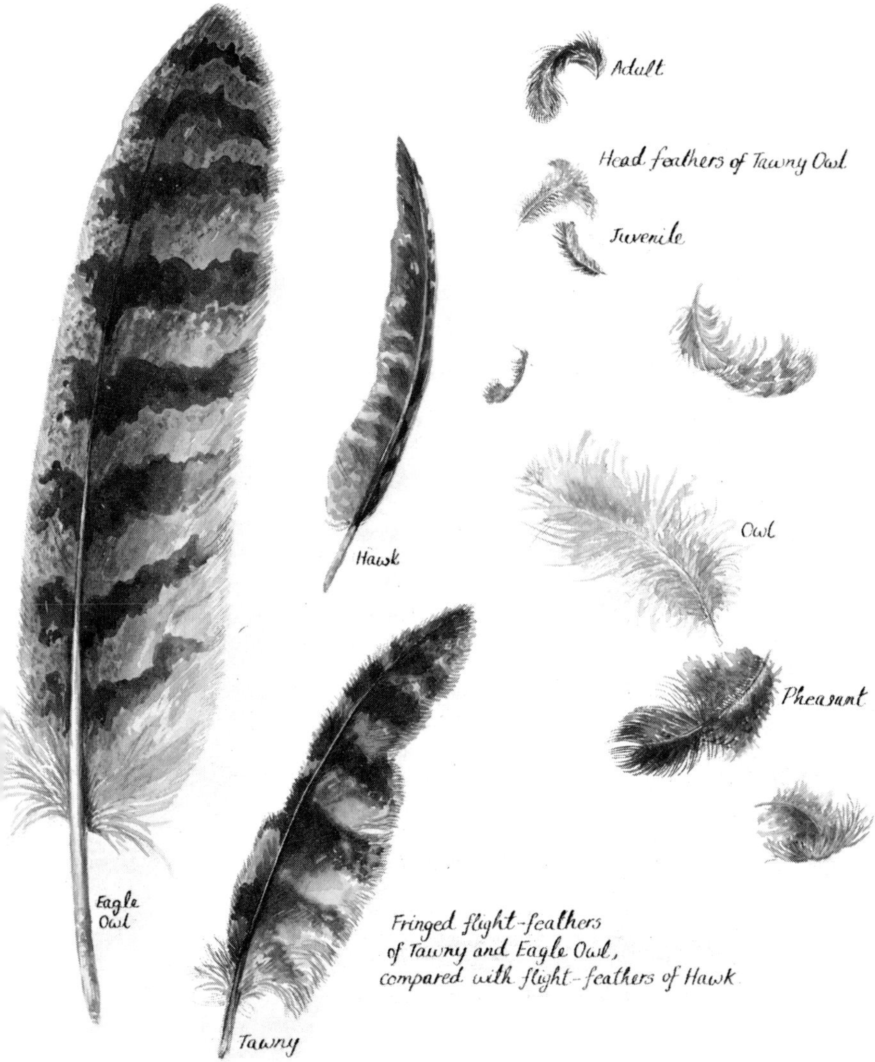
Adult
Head feathers of Tawny Owl
Juvenile
Hawk
Owl
Pheasant
Eagle Owl
Fringed flight-feathers of Tawny and Eagle Owl, compared with flight-feathers of Hawk
Tawny

feathers began to drop. A few fell from the back, and after a while things really got under way. First, the leading primaries, the largest of the flight feathers, were shed—always in pairs, one from each side, so that although flying may be a little more difficult, the owl is never off balance to impair accuracy in catching its food. When all these feathers had been replaced, the tail was shed—quickly. Its function is steering and maintaining balanced flight, and rapid growth ensures that within three weeks there is a workable rudder back again. So important is the tail, this vital steering device, that after the age of two the tawny only sheds it every other year. Last year Chippy had a bath, shook himself, and his entire tail dropped on the floor! It was so sudden that for a little while he had difficulty in flying. With no brakes he overshot the edge of the shelf and hit the wall. He tried to compensate, then undershot and fell off twice before getting the hang of it. His appearance at this stage of the moult was slightly comical because without the dignity of a tail, from the back he looked exactly like a large brown beetle.

Next to go were the secondaries which give lift, hence a period of rather more noisy flight. Then the tertiaries fell. These are the few flight feathers between the wing proper and the body. At the same time he had also been losing feathers from his chest, those beautiful white and cream waistcoat feathers tipped with a broad arrow-mark. By June the floor each morning was littered not only with paper which he had torn up, and wool and string plucked from his toys, but also with feathers—everywhere.

Up until this stage all this had not made much difference to his appearance—except when he had no tail—but gradually the facial disk began to lose its distinctive patterning and turned almost grey. Before long one could see new quills coming through, giving him a rather sad, moth-eaten expression, with bare patches round the eyes. Slowly the tiny quill cases burst, revealing bright new feathers of cream, russet, white and fawn—and a more cheerful-looking bird. Almost the last to be shed were the alula feathers, which, short vaned and strong, correspond to our thumbs, and are used to prevent stalling and speed up the flow of air over the wings. A sigh of relief from me—it was almost over. But I had forgotten that the underwing also had to be replaced (more work for the carpet sweeper in the mornings). These feathers are short, broad, and white; marked to give a distinctive barred pattern on the underside of the wings. Oh yes, and last to go were a few fine, long 'lingerie' feathers from under the tail. Then behold—a new owl in his full glory.

Apart from the housework, there is another reason why I am glad when moulting is over. In the wild there are plenty of moths and beetles to be caught which provide roughage and give the extra nourishment that the owl needs for making new feathers, and one has to be very careful with the feeding of a resident bird of prey at this time. Extra vitamins are supplied each week with a smear of Abidec on the food, and rather than give tablets, I make sure that there is plenty of pounded up chicken neck to supply calcium, along with liver and as many mice as we can catch. Wolly would eat plenty of liver, but Chippy is not so keen on it, and if too much is taken at one time it is inclined to upset his tummy. The danger of not providing correct food during this time is that any deficiency would show up as hunger-trace; a hair-line of weakness across the new feathers with the consequent risk of their breaking under strain, and they cannot be replaced until the moult the following year.

I collect and keep all the discarded feathers. Children and adults like to take some as a souvenir of their visits here—we have even had a request from Canada for some. I never cease to marvel at the variety and infinite beauty of this cast-off clothing of the owls, and often take out the box to have a look at them. They are all there, from tiny face feathers like minute herring bones, which laid on top of each other give the effect of fine silk gauze, to the big flight feathers that have a soft thick covering of velvet pile on their upper surface and delicate fringed edges, which combine to deaden the sound of air flowing over them and make for silent flight. The owl has comparatively short, rounded wings, which are very broad and give it buoyancy and lift, so that it can fly at almost stalling speed, hovering like a kestrel before pouncing. But owls can fly like rockets when they've a mind to, and move too fast for the eye to follow. Tawny owls are birds of the woodland and seldom go far from it, so they have to be able to manouvre fast amongst the branches and be capable of great speed over short distances. They do not always fly silently though. Bird language is expressed not only by voice, and angry owls, just like robins and other small birds, can use their wings to give vent to their feelings. With feathers turned slightly so that the air rushes past the vanes, they can flutter about making as much noise as a startled chicken when occasion demands.

After gliding as silently as a ghost and alighting as softly as one of their own feathers, they can sometimes land with a flat-footed crash that shakes the place. Often when I am resting on the couch I cover my feet with a thick blanket and wiggle my toes about. This is the game of mouse-finding, and Chippy is a past master at it. He will adopt the cautious approach, moving closer and closer until only a short hop away. It is the silent pause between movement that attracts, and he has endless patience; but when he judges the right moment has come, he jumps, hovering above my feet for the space of three wing-beats, then with legs held stiffly out and claws at the attack position, he lands like a falling brick, and instantly the full crushing power of his talons is applied, once, twice. If my foot had been a mouse, it would at once have met its ancestors. Occasionally those sharp claws will penetrate the blanket and . . . OUCH!

10

Modifications

The studio has been modified for the safety and convenience of its feathered occupants, and by watching them as they grew I've been able to add several improvements for their comfort. Extra grip-ledges have been screwed to the window sills and tops of the bookcases. The casing of the sunblind has been covered in, partly to stop the cords being chewed through, but mainly because once Squeaky got hung up there by her claws. The light switches to the overhead tube-lights have had to be taped over—Chippy can turn the lights on, but he can't turn them off again! I have strategically placed pictures on the walls, so that by looking at the reflections in the glass, Owl on his shelf can, without bothering to move, keep a watch on what is going on outside. By this method he can literally see what goes on behind his back. The picture framès are also ideal for landing on and swinging from at night, and in the morning they are usually hanging at odd angles. All wooden ledges have been carefully sanded, and perches covered in cloth for better grip.

Not every room has rather shredded perches stuck round the place, but although I have seen visitors look at them, no one has asked why they are there. The thing that does surprise me is that some have remarked how tidy the place is (which doesn't say much for the reputation of artists in general!) but I have never been able to work in untidy surroundings, and in any case, have enough clearing up in the mornings without having extra clutter on which a bird could hurt itself.

One morning I noticed a tiny speck of blood on the new grip-ledge on top of the bookcase; and the ensuing conversation (with a bit of imagination), went something like this . . .

'Wake up a minute. There's something I want to see.'

'Go away . . . I'm sleeping.'

Upheaval while owl is removed from shelf and put on my lap.

'Oh no . . . not beak clipping time again?'

'No, I want to look at your feet.'

'Why? Oh well—if you must—here's one.'

Pause for examination.

'Nothing there. Please let me have the other.'

'No.'

'YES.' (Grabbing the foot.) 'Now open it.'

'NO.'

'Ooh look!—what's that outside?'

'If it's that cat again . . . let me see!' and while he concentrates on the possibility of Cat going near his mousetrap, a finger is deftly inserted between claws to open the clenched foot.

'Aha. I thought so—a splinter.'

Attention comes back to what is going on.

'It doesn't hurt really—I was only sliding on the. . . .'

'Yes, I know what you were doing. How did you manage that? I sandpapered the wood most carefully.'

'Well, there *was* this one little bit left sticking up . . . .'

'No there wasn't—but I'd forgotten you carry your own sharpeners around with you' (meanwhile extracting splinter and dressing with antiseptic cream).

'Oooh that feels better. But it was that new bit—simply asked to be skated on. Your fault really.'

It usually is!

The tray on the highest bookcase is a recent innovation. Up to now, the owl-bath was a thick glass bowl, but Chippy got so big that it became useless for more than a face wash. We searched in many shops without success for something large enough (much to the amusement of the staff when they learned why we wanted it), until we found just the thing at a garden centre—a plastic gravel-tray for flower pots. Two feet long by fourteen inches wide and not too deep, with a stepping stone at one end it makes an ideal bath; Chippy can't upset it and has plenty of room for his swimming routine. The wall alongside has been covered with waterproof material (something else that makes a good ripping noise when pulled off by a sharp beak!). The installation of the new bath was watched with great interest, and of course had to be inspected and tested. There was just one slight complaint, that 'one's claws were inclined to slip a little on the plastic rim', which was soon taken care of by applying drafting tape over the offending area, and Chippy returned to roost and dream of the forthcoming delights of a real lie-down bath that night. He was still asleep when a friend called. All was peace until she put out a hand to admire the new bath. Instantly Chippy was awake. 'Leave that alone!' he shrieked from the shelf, 'That's *mine*', and like a rocket he shot across the room to land on the edge of the new bath and glare

at her, wings held out in anger. That evening he not only put water on the floor and up the wall, but managed to wet the ceiling as well. The new bath was an unqualified success.

Another thing that had to be altered was the shelf. It had to be made wider and lowered to give him more room.

And why is it that most of my polite requests turn into king-size arguments?

'Please move off, I want to unscrew your shelf.' That apparently didn't go in. I should know better than to ask such a thing in the morning when he was resting from having kept me awake all night. So I climbed onto a chair and removed all the play-things stored around him. Not much notice taken, as this is all part of the usual procedure of checking to see if he has overlooked the odd piece of beef. One velvet mouse . . . three red chocolate papers . . . one . . . ah, I wondered where that had gone to—my best eraser! And—you blighter—do you know how much sable brushes cost these days? One beak sharpening twig, well gnawed. One . . . good grief . . . whats *that*? Ugh—how long have you had that up here? This last remark is treated with lofty disdain. Then I had to start unscrewing the holding brackets with his weight still pressing them down. The shelf began to loosen and wobble and it suddenly dawned on him what was going on. As the last screw was withdrawn and he found himself coming down, still sitting there, he just couldn't believe that I would be capable of such perfidy as to remove his private sanctum. Up went all the feathers, and going to the centre perch, surprise written all over his face, he watched in amazement as I laid the shelf on the table and began to work on it. Perhaps I had not yet realized the enormity of what I'd done? To make it perfectly plain to me, he deliberately flew up to the place where the shelf had been, hit the wall and landed on the floor with a hoot of indignation. I took no notice but went on with what I was doing. This was too much. He landed with a thud on the table, wings out, claws wrenching the screwdriver out of my hand.

'Look,' I tried to explain, putting him on my shoulder, 'you'll have to WAIT. I'm trying to make it bigger for you.'

'Why? It's all right as it is!'

'No it isn't. The text books say you should be fifteen inches long with a wingspan of under three feet. Look at you—over eighteen inches and wings like an eagle owl!'

'What's a text book know about anything? It says I eat shrews too. Huh! nonsense.'

'Now. GET OFF IT—and just WAIT and see'. He marches impatiently up and down my back as I fit the new extension and move the brackets.

'Now, let's put it back for you.' And if you've ever been helped by a full-grown tawny, you might think of many things easier to do than hold a two foot long plank up near the ceiling, plus the screw steady, and try to keep the screwdriver in the slot, without beating wings, scrabbling claws and rude comments getting in the way. But we finally got the job done. Chippy retreated to get a better look. The feathers went down.

'Well? Aren't you going back on it? All that fuss over nothing.'

'Now just hold on there, wait a minute—it's different—can't just go rushing back—it might bite me or something.' While I clear up the tools, Chippy thinks about it, then flies up to land gingerly on the edge.

'Hey, that's better—much more room now—Oh yes I like it.' Pause. 'Where are my TOYS? You've moved them!' Everything is counted as it is replaced—then: 'What about THAT? I kept it in case I might be hungry one day.'

'That'll be the day when you'll ever feel hungry enough to eat that—anyway owls don't eat biltong—and this revolting thing is being thrown OUT.'

I sometimes wonder why I don't just take up something peaceful—like lion taming!

11

Flight paths

There is an old oak tree across the road near the farm next to us, and halfway up its massive trunk is a hole where the barn owls nest. Each year all through the June evenings, starting promptly at a quarter past nine, the parent birds hunt over the lane that leads to our cottage. This roadway is unsurfaced, with banks and ditches on either side and overhung by trees. Down this green tunnel, at ten minute intervals until after dark comes one of the great white birds, gliding slowly along on hardly moving wings, about five feet above the ground. One can so clearly see the golden patterning on its back and the head swinging from side to side as dark eyes scan the ground beneath. We are hidden away from the rest of the village, and the lane, or droveway, ends at a field gate just beyond the house, so there is no traffic to disturb the owls. They are so used to me that they do not deviate from their flight path even if I happen to be standing near. Knowing where the nest was, I was interested to see if I could trace the path of the hunting birds.

Over the years, having to go out each night to feed my charges, my night vision has improved enormously and most of the time I don't even bother to switch on the dim light in the studio. Often when out in the evenings people have asked me to wait while they switched on a light so that I could see my way. This has led to a remark I often use now, 'Us owls can see in the dark!' And I can, for there are in the country very few nights in the year when all is pitch black. And there are tricks that can be used to help the vision at night. If one sits, or lies prone with one's face close to the earth, the range of vision is immediately lengthened, because peering along the ground the faintly luminous sky serves as a background and anything moving against it will show up. Another trick is to stare, not focusing on any thing in particular, keeping the head still; then any movement, no matter how slight, within one's binocular range will instantly register on the retina. The barn owls were easy to follow because their white colouring showed up well, and also the timing of their sorties was so regular. To see where they turned, say, at the corner of a field, it was easy to wait there until they came round again, then go on to wait at the next angle of their flight. In this way I found that each sortie went for just over a quarter of a mile. One would fly past the house, over two fields, past the vicarage garden, over the churchyard (there at least I had a gravestone to lean against while waiting), along two hedgerows, and back to the nest. Each time the bird picked up something along the way. The other parent bird took a path over the farmyard, an orchard, our garden, and down the field hedgerows to the river and back.

The tawnies have a different method of hunting. Rather than using a set route, they locate places where prey is most likely to be found and wait quietly in the trees until something moves on the ground below. Then having exhausted the supply there for a while they move on to another place. Thus the hunting of the tawny is

more selective, and covers a different area pattern than does that of a barn owl. If I happen to locate a tawny while I am out after dusk I always keep well away so as not to disturb it. My being near does not upset the barn owls because the area they cover is so much bigger. The tawnies, Britain's largest indigenous owl, are bigger and more belligerent than the white owls, and they seem to have staked a permanent claim to the farm rickyards—otherwise the two don't interfere with each other's hunting rights. This truce only lasts for about six weeks each year when they are first feeding their young: after that we don't see the barn owls again until the following June. Their winter territory is over common scrub-land and woods half a mile away from us.

The third type of owl we have nearby is the little owl, *Athene noctua*, called by some locals 'the French owl'. It is a shy, secretive little bird, only eight and a half inches high. Unlike the tawny and barn owls with dark eyes, the little owl has bright yellow ones with black pupils, set under bushy white eyebrows in a broad flat head. Little owls are beautifully coloured, with white bars and splotches on their soft brown plumage. Although they can take prey as big as a rat, they do a lot of their hunting on the ground where they pick up worms, insects and beetles, devouring many craneflies, or daddy-long-legs, which are the larvae of the leather-jacket; so the little owls are a great help to farmers. They are not strictly nocturnal and can sometimes be seen in the daytime sitting on overhead wires by the roadside.

Britain has five indigenous owls: the tawny—or brown or wood-owl, the barn owl and little owl, and the long and short-eared owls. The last two do not live around here, as the long-eared owl prefers conifer and forest land and the short-eared owl is a bird of open, marshy ground. Incidentally, the ears are nothing to do with their actual hearing, but tufts of feathers that have led to them being so named. Scientists are still arguing over whether these feather tufts do in fact assist the hearing by deflecting sound to the ears, or if they are merely used in display or as recognition symbols. The ear tufts on these and the eagle owls can be raised or lowered at will.

A great tragedy, not only for the owls but for all the birds, was the advent of the terrible elm disease. In the West country alone we have lost several million trees. Most of the big trees around here were elms, and for the past two years we have been living to the noise of chain-saws as the dead trees are felled and cleared. Now we have views across the countryside that we had not been able to see before.

During the two successive years' drought when the disease struck we fed the garden birds all summer: there was no natural food and no water for them. Even the river dried up. I have managed to half tame a family of carrion crows who will come to the lawn to be fed, but already rooks and jackdaws are far less numerous than they were a few years ago.

With mechanized farming, new roads and fast expanding villages and the removal of miles of hedgerows, the countryside has changed enormously since we came here nearly twenty years ago—and not for the better. What many people don't realize is that the trees provide moisture and oxygen to the air we breathe, and the loss of such a vast number is going to change our climate and affect our already inadequate water supply. To us perhaps, the effect of the prolonged drought was not too immediate, but for wild creatures it was drastic and in some cases, final. Since then we have had plenty of rain

but the water table is still not back to its previous level. That may take years yet. The row of elms that stood beyond our garden is no longer there, so the tawnies have moved away to nest in the oak wood beyond the river. I think this is one of the reasons why Chippy has now turned his attention and affection more closely towards me. Before, his pals were here almost every night for a talk or noisy arguments, but now they do not come so frequently.

There is something I would like to add here.

If you are out walking in the woods or fields and find a baby owl on the ground . . . PLEASE, leave it alone. Young owls spend a lot of their time on the ground and are perfectly safe from most predators . . . except humans. If danger threatens, a three-week-old tawny is quite capable of climbing right up the trunk of a tree, using its beak and claws as climbing hooks. It can go fast too. Owls are protected birds and may not be kept in cages. So, if you see them, look and marvel, but leave them alone. The only time they might need your help is if they are obviously injured. Take them first to a vet, who will advise you, then as soon as possible after recovery they should be returned to where they were found.

And another plea. If you do find yourself having to care for a bird of prey—any bird of prey, do not feed them on bread and milk or give raw spirits, as I have known some do . . . it will kill them. For the young, chunky dog-meat from a tin will make a good meal, and worms or small pieces of raw meat. Not everyone has a supply of feathers or fur to wrap the food in, so very short pieces of wool will do, or even tiny bits of shredded string (natural fibres, not the plastic sort), and again, certainly *not* human hair, for roughage.

If you are feeding wild birds only put out peanuts for the small ones in winter, never in the spring. If a tit takes nuts to her brood she will unintentionally kill them all. The best food for small birds is grated or chopped cheese mixed with dripping and breakfast porridge oats. This is the nearest thing to their natural food, and the little birds will be safe.

12

Fed by an owl

I am continually surprised at all the wonderful things that have happened since I have been living near owls. But now, and I can still hardly believe it, I have been fed by an owl.

I had better explain how this came about.

For many years I have been a glass-engraver. Using diamond points and diamond drills, everything from goblets to church windows in crystal have gone out all over the world. Glass dust and chips in the studio did not bother me, but with the coming of Wolly, this definitely had to stop. Glass is far too dangerous to have around, because no matter how carefully one cleaned up after work there was always the risk that a living creature might pick up slivers of glass, the real danger being that one can't always see them. As his well-being was more important than any work of mine, I gave it up and concentrated on painting and drawing. But later on, getting bored with doing the same sort of thing all the time, it gave me a chance to try something new. So I turned to wood carving. Now our usually tidy studio is more like a glory-hole workshop, especially at moulting time when there are shavings, chips, sawdust and feathers all over the place. Chippy, now well named, doesn't mind how much noise I make with mallet and chisels; the only thing that neither of us care for much is rip-sawing. Cutting along the grain of a big plank is hard work, and after a while the vibration gets on the nerves of both of us. However, in fine weather I do most of the sawing outside. I cannot have big power tools in the studio because of the noise they make, but to help the work along I have an electric bench-grinder. At one end of it is a silicon-carbide wheel for sharpening tools and the chuck at the other end takes sanding disks. The motor runs very sweetly with rather a pleasing hum, and I had got into the habit, after switching off, of using my finger to slow down and stop the spindle turning. That came after nearly catching my nose on the still turning abrasive wheel, and at three thousand revs. per minute it wasn't calculated to improve my appearance very much.

I think what started it all off was that my finger used as a brake must have made a slight squeaking noise. Chippy woke, then as I continued to work, he came down to his feeding place, grabbed a small piece of meat left over from his last meal, slammed down onto my shoulder and chittering loudly, held the meat without swallowing it. He shook it, still not eating. Naturally my concern was for him. Was his beak too long? Had it impaled the meat? I sat him on my lap to have a closer look. But his beak looked perfectly all right so I let him go. The next time I stopped the machine the same thing happened. Again he grabbed the food and landed with a crash on my shoulder. Again he would neither swallow or let go of the meat. This time I told him to stop messing about and let me get on with my work. He went back to his shelf to think things over. I could almost hear him doing it, as with both feet down and wings slightly drooping, he stared hard at the wall. Then, as temper hadn't worked he tried the gentle approach. Again he picked up his bit of meat, but this time landing very softly, he leaned over and offered me the mouthful. At last, and how slow witted he must have thought me, I realized what he was doing, and accepted his gift. He watched closely as I pretended to eat, and then hid the meat in my pocket, as I dare not let him see me put it down. Satisfied, he got the rest of the beef and fed it to me until it was all gone and then returned to his shelf. I was so tickled with this performance that the following day I called John, and again stopped the sander with my finger to see what would happen. At once, down came Chippy, and again I was fed. Now, being rather a softie, I often spend time with sandpaper and files instead of using the machine, so as not to disturb Chippy when he is having a sleep!

But more remarkable still was another feeding incident, and this had nothing to do with any sound that I may have made. It was an example of pure mind reading, which I have referred to earlier.

Unfortunately, I have osteo-arthritis in both knees, and when the weather is about to change, then I know all about it. One night recently was one of those times. Rain was on the way, and I knew I was in for a rough night when pain would keep me awake, so rather than disturb John I took my blankets out to the studio, where if I couldn't sleep at least I could have coffee from the thermos and a cigarette, or perhaps read to pass the time along. That night Chippy had a mouse. Usually as soon as he is hungry he eats it whole, but this evening he spent a long time pottering about with it, and I couldn't make out what he was doing. The weather was turning cold, and I hurt. Badly. It took me ages to get reasonably comfortable and drop off into an uneasy sleep, with Chippy still fidgeting about up on his shelf. Suddenly I was woken by a soft *purrp*. I hadn't felt him land, but he was on my chest offering me his mouse! He was holding it by the tail, and then I realized what he had been doing. The head had been taken off and the rest gutted and cleaned. Gently he came nearer, holding it out with another soft sound. Half awake, it was difficult to know what to do, as I was completely overcome by the love and sympathy he showed me in offering me the most precious thing he had. All I could do was thank him and touch the mouse. 'But,' I said, 'to make me better . . . you eat it for me.' He must have understood, because he flew back and in two quick gulps . . . the mouse had gone.

After that I don't think anything would surprise me again. It was worth a bit of pain just to have such a rare and wonderful thing happen. One of those occasions which make us realize just how deep are love and understanding when we share our lives with the living creatures around us. And it further explains how impatient I get when people still believe silly nonsense about 'owls being of ill omen'. And I also become angry when creatures are treated in an anthropomorphic way. The dictionary defines that word as 'ascription of human faculties to the lower animals'. Lower indeed! They could teach us a lot, without us heaping this final insult on them.

John is one of those unfortunate people who react badly to insect bites; so badly that I think two wasp stings would put him in hospital. During the prolonged drought there was an absolute plague of wasps, and try as I might I couldn't locate all the nests. Then help came from an unexpected quarter. A badger turned up each night, found the nests and dug them out, enabling me to destroy the residue in the morning. He found six in the garden and two more big ones in the drove. But if I get nervous for John with wasps around, that's nothing to what I feel about hornets, and when the wind is blowing south from the hills we sometimes get them here. It is no good swatting at them and hoping they will go away, because if one gets good and mad, it will chase you. So with them constantly at the back of my mind in summer, I did not delay long the day I saw something big flying round above the lawn. Arming myself with a folded newspaper I went out to investigate. It landed on a bush. But when I drew near, I saw it wasn't a hornet. It was a huge wood-wasp fully two inches long. The body was bright orange, banded with black, and I was able to get near enough to see its bright, glittering eyes watching me. It had wings like a bumble bee, only much bigger, and a long ovipositor, and I was able to study it for quite some time before it flew away.

I looked it up in a book and found it was the Great Wood Horntail, one of the most beautiful insects I have ever seen, and even for John, that was one I wasn't going to kill.

Recently I was making a carving of a snail and became engrossed with their sinuous shapes and beauty of form, so got out the encyclopedia and began to read about them. And I had a surprise. I had always thought that all slugs were pests in a garden, but learned that it is only the smaller ones which eat the plants. The huge ones which come trundling out after rain looking as though they are going to chop down the nearest tree, only feed on decaying material and fungi. I have been doing them injustice all these years . . . poor things.

Chippy, watching everything I do, doesn't miss a thing, so when I make a carving of a mouse I hide it if I leave the studio. He has already carried away two of them, one losing its tail when he found that they were made of wood and couldn't be eaten. But once he was a very puzzled owl. I was writing out posters for a local craft show, and with them were some arrows—black on yellow card—which, when they were done, were put on the couch for the ink to dry. Down flew Chippy. Ignoring the posters, he went for the arrows and was busy trying to scrape them off with his claws. It was then that I saw that the shape of an arrow, seen from above, is the shape that an owl recognizes as a mouse, the dart of the arrow being the ears. Poor Chippy, he couldn't make out why they would not come off the card, so I made him one and cut it out and he took it and put it amongst his toys. I had always believed that it was the movement of the mouse that betrayed it, but here was an owl demonstrating that even if the mouse kept utterly still, its very shape would be a dead giveaway . . . and I do mean dead.

Recently we had a wood-burning stove installed in the living room to replace an electric fire. The great old chimney had been capped for several years to stop jackdaws dropping twigs down it at nesting time, and now the asbestos cover had to be taken off and replaced by a stone slab resting on bricks. That way the chimney could function properly but it would still frustrate the building proclivities of the birds. A heavy stone slab had to go up on the roof, but as the slates and stringers would not bear such weight, John told the workmen to go up via the studio roof. Chippy wouldn't tolerate men walking about on *his* roof, so I carried him upstairs and parked him in my bedroom while work was going on. The men were fascinated to be watched by an owl sitting in the half open window, and that didn't help the work along as they kept stopping to talk to him. However, as soon as the capping was in place and the ladders down I brought Chippy out again. With him in my arms we passed the foreman who was standing outside. Round came Chippy's head and he let out such a *clack* . . . even the foreman knew what that loud cracking sound meant: 'Go AWAY. You're disrupting my peace' or something less polite.

He was vastly amused. 'Often get cussed at,' he grinned 'but never by an owl before!'

13

Of hawks and mice

Sometimes it is not the sounds one hears so much as sounds one doesn't, that alert the never-sleeping sixth sense to the fact that something is wrong. Total concentration on work is also total awareness of what is going on around. The mind has catalogued and taken into account all the natural noises of the day, and ignoring them, is not disturbed: a twig falling on the roof; the fence creaking as a cow reaches under to scratch her neck on the rail; a tractor engine starting up with a roar; or the garden birds busy with food put out for them, twittering and squabbling over bits of fat and cheese.

Suddenly the alarm bell of the mind rings. Triggered not by sound but silence. No noise where there should be noise. Usually when the birds are quiet it means that there is a hawk waiting overhead. But this time when I went to look, the sky was clear of any flying shape. No sound—nothing moved anywhere. The place down the path where the food is put out was deserted. Oats still lay scattered on the feeding table and on the ground by a big old-fashioned rose bush. Then as I stood, puzzled, I realized that the bush was crammed with birds—finches, robins, tits, sparrows—all tensed, but utterly still. Under them on the ground, half hidden by a clump of plants, I could see part of the tail of a large bird in the shadows. Sometimes the eye sees but the brain is not quick to comprehend something out of the ordinary. My first thought was that this must be an injured bird, a pigeon perhaps, lying there. I stepped onto the flower bed and put out a hand, but as I did the bird moved; and at once I knew what had happened. There was a hawk, though not where I'd expected one, and I had almost touched it. I stood where I was, keeping absolutely still. It was so occupied that it was quite oblivious of my presence. It sprang up and around, spiralling to the top of the bush. As the hawk rose, the small birds hurtled down to crouch on the ground—heads tilted, bright eyes watching. It flung itself off; flying round and down: the birds like a counter balance streaking up to safety in the prickled mat of twigs and leaf covering above.

It was a sparrowhawk, a beautiful male. I could see black whiskers standing stiffly round the hooked beak, light and dark yellow streaking the wild furious eyes, the clenching of nervous feet, the shine and polish of black talons. He craned his neck sideways, peering into the branches above, uttering a harsh *kerrk* of temper and frustration as he launched himself to crash-land on top of the bush again. Instantly the small birds dropped like falling water, out of reach. Again he flung his broad, arrow shape in a tight circle round the bush—the wind of his passing brushing my hand—to land at my feet, legs spread, wings mantled, body panting in anger. He made a sideways lunge, stumbling over my foot, only to be brought up sharply by a prickle-branch that barred the way to the birds, now spooled tightly round the centre of the rose bush like a quivering coloured thread. Twice more, fury concentrated in those blazing eyes, he tried unsuccessfully to reach them, before, in sympathy with his predicament I laughed. 'You'll never catch them that way old son!' The hawk turned, surprise taking the place of anger. For the span of two heartbeats our eyes held each other, then without haste he flew away to the flat roof of the garage, where he turned, feathers roused, to glare at us. The little birds sat tight. I went indoors to get some strips of fresh beef from Chippy's food in the fridge and threw them up on the roof. The hawk had moved into a tree, but stayed to watch, and as soon as I had gone back inside came to take the meat. But it was quite some time after he had gone away over the farm buildings before the other birds came out to finish their food.

A pair of sparrowhawks often come here in the winter and we put bones and scraps out for them; and quite often they will raid the bird table. Twice we have been lucky enough to see the mighty peregrines as they pass over on their way south in October. We were going up to the hills once when John suddenly stopped the car. Sitting on the top branch of a small tree not far from the road was a huge hawk. By its size, it was the peregrine falcon, the female. (The male is called the tiercel, because he is a third smaller than she is: fifteen inches long to her nineteen inches.) We were so close that we could see clearly the slate-grey back, the distinctive barring on the chest, the yellow cere of the beak, the big dark eyes, and the strong yellow feet. We watched, and she looked at us for a few minutes before taking off over the trees. Shortly after, when we got out of the car on top of the hill, there she was again, riding the thermals in lazy circles. With her were three kestrels, looking like attendant fighter planes escorting a great bomber. We looked until they drifted away and were lost to sight in the distant haze. I treasure the memory of that afternoon. The second time I saw a peregrine I happened to look up and saw one right above the garden. It was hovering on outstretched wings with finger-tip ends curled slightly upward. As I stood, it came a bit lower, watching me. I lifted an arm in salute, and instantly it jinked, flinching slightly. It was that 'reaching out through space' that made it a personal thing between us—the reaction of the hawk to my movement, as though it had been within easy reach. Slowly it circled and then flew away while I watched until my eyes ached against the glare of the cool autumn sky.

*   *

John had been working in the garden and we were sitting outside having a cup of tea when he said, 'Don't move—look at those birds over there.' On the newly dug vegetable bed were five starlings and a mouse. As we watched, two of the birds got between the mouse and the ditch, heading it off when it ran that way, the rest forming a circle which closed around it until the running mouse came to a halt. Then swiftly one pounced, pecking at the little creature, the rest joining in. The dead mouse was picked up and they all flew off. It was the only time that we have seen anything like that, and the way in which the birds worked together without a sound, was intriguing to watch.

Among our garden birds, one of them, a great tit, was an individualist—or just greedier than the rest. Scorning to feed with the others he would spend his days flying along the house to see which room we were in, and would then bang on the windows until we were forced to give him cheese just to stop his importuning. John called him 'Hogbird', and it was impossible to ignore him, as he would follow wherever we went. He even made the mistake of coming into the studio. Suddenly he saw the owl and made a dash for freedom, only to find the window shut. Owl and I made for him at the same moment, but luckily I got there a split second ahead, and as my hands closed over him Chippy landed hard on top. Hogbird, chastened by that experience, confined his efforts to coming into the house whenever he could find a way, and we were constantly having to catch and put him out again. But one day—no Hogbird, and when I next went out, there was Chippy with a smug expression, and underneath on the floor, a pathetic pile of tit tail-feathers.

Our black cat often brought me a mouse that she had caught as a present, but once she carried things too far. Trotting in from the garden she laid a live mouse at my feet. I appreciated the gift but that was not quite the right place for it, and while we chased it round and round the living room, she sat in the doorway enjoying the fun. The mouse disappeared. We moved furniture, looked under the couch, searched the fireplace, and generally turned the place upside down. When the room was a thorough wreck, we both happened to look up at the same time and there it was, perched on top of the television set unconcernedly washing its whiskers. This time all three of us converged on it. The mouse watched us come with beady-eyed interest, then at the last moment, streaked down the aerial cable and vanished into thin air. We never saw it again.

Can you imagine anything more frustrating than to hear at one a.m., a mouse wearing hobnail boots, scrunching away at the woodwork behind a wall only a

few inches from Owl and myself? The house was full with guests staying over Christmas, and I had to seek a bed with Chippy out in the studio. I was tired out by all the preparations for the next day's party, and everything was peaceful until the mouse started up in the small hours. He came clattering along a joist to stop just beside where I lay, and started gnawing loudly. Chippy hooted and landed on the bed. I banged the wall with my fist.

It had no effect. Mouse crunched on without even pausing. Chippy shrieked and clawed the wall. I banged harder. Mouse stamped, moved a few inches, and began his second course on a new bit of wood. Chippy landed on top of my head to get a bit nearer, wings beating and claws slipping and sliding in my hair. That was the *end*. Half asleep, I gathered up my blankets and came back into the house, leaving the two of them to get on with it. Forlornly I stood clutching my bedclothes, looking at the couch—which was too short to lie on, and my arm chair—which was occupied by the cat, who refused to move. I directed some very unkind thoughts at the person who now slumbered peacefully in my comfortable bed upstairs! Wearily spreading my things on the floor I knew exactly how that square peg in its round hole must have felt. But worse was to come. When I finally dozed off, the cat decided that I looked a softer prospect and deserted the chair to park her heavy self on top of me before resuming her untroubled sleep. Needless to say, I was not exactly in the mood for goodwill to all men, when I surfaced stiff and cramped on Christmas morning.

On a cold February night as midnight approached I was relaxing in my armchair by the fire when I heard a crash outside and the sound of falling glass. I rushed to the studio, and there, like two naughty kids caught stealing apples, were the owls. Chippy inside, and on the window sill outside, a wild tawny. Between them was the window with a big hole in it. They both looked surprised and at the same time very guilty. Neither moved as I went over to them; luckily the only casualty was the window pane. There was broken glass everywhere. The wild one didn't fly away until I began to pick up the pieces outside. As the window couldn't be left like that with jagged bits of glass sticking out of the frame, I put plastic sheeting over the hole, pinning it down securely. This didn't please Chippy at all, and for the next few days until we got it mended, he grumbled at me because he couldn't see out. The front wall is all windows, but no, *he* wanted to look out of the small side window just because it was covered up, and he kept on and on niggling at me until in the end it was one occasion when I had to use a firm and final NO. He gave in with very bad grace until the day a new pane was put back, and all was peace again.

Friends from London say, 'It must be very boring in the country in the winter.' If they only knew! For like the elephant's child, owls are full of 'satiable curiosity', and whatever is going on they want a piece of the action, so there is not often a dull moment.

* *

If I may be allowed to strike a more serious note. Rewarding as it has been for me, I will not pretend for one moment that this 'owl project' has been easy. Nor was it undertaken in a light-hearted manner. It was started because I could not bear the thought of one small orphan from the wild having no place to go; and it was successful, partly because I have had to make over my life-style to fit in with those under my care. To the annoyance of some of my friends I have become almost a recluse; holidays are out of the question, so is any trip that would keep me away for more than a few hours at a time. During the summer I do not leave at all, as to shut the studio would be impossible. I am lucky in having a big airy studio, and in the work I do—also in the place where we live; all this has helped, but I was not joking when I said that I had become part owl. Complete understanding of them and their ways is a prerequisite for standing *in loco parentis*; for we are not here dealing with an earth-bound creature, but one whose very life is in the feeling of air under its wings, which should know no restraint in any form, but whose freedom depends on one knowing how and when to introduce it back into the wild. I have never even thought of the cost of feeding the owls, but over the years it must have been quite considerable. Some people may think all this, just to be able to hear a hoot from the dark outside, may sound a bit crazy. But to me that sound is something right in this topsy-turvy world, and if I never did anything else in my life, that free hoot would be the one thing that justified my existence.

14

Full circle

My owl-project has become known in the area, and now people bring me injured birds they have found. I hate the carnage to wild creatures caused by traffic on busy roads, and with birds, unless the injury is slight, often wish it had been an outright kill. Better that than the almost hopeless job of trying to return a handicapped one to the wild. My first question on hearing of anyone finding an injured bird or animal is, 'Have you taken it to a vet?' That is the first thing that should be done, and I am always astonished that it seems to be the last thing so many think about. Over the years I have handled many injured birds and have worked closely with our vet, caring for them after he has treated them and dressed their wounds.

One bird in particular I remember. When Chippy was two years old, late one Sunday evening neighbours came to bring an owl that had flown into the windscreen of their car. Although they were not going fast, they said the impact was like a bomb going off, and had at once stopped and picked up the injured bird and brought it straight here. This was a little owl, the goddess Pallas Athene's own special symbol, but now more dead than alive, except for his blazing black-pupilled yellow eyes.

As he was handed gently to me, one small leg hung broken and useless. We put on a bandage to straighten the injury and keep it clean, and then I held him close to me under the warmth of a woollen jacket. For four hours I held him, listening fearfully to every breath that rasped and bubbled in his throat, willing with all my strength to make him well. Gradually the breathing quietened and slowed, and the owl moved in my hand, seeking a more comfortable position. He was over the initial shock and would live at least until the morning.

I kept him near me all night on a soft towel in a large box by my bed, and next morning we took him to the vet, who splinted the broken bone, padding and covering the injury. It couldn't have happened in a worse place. Instead of a clean cut higher up the leg, this was a jagged break just above the foot at the ankle, where it would be difficult to prevent the foot twisting as it healed. Home again, the little owl settled down in one corner of his box, his slight weight lying on a foam-rubber cushion covered with a soft cloth, and he was left to rest. I had put the box on its side, the front covered with an old metal cake-rack, so that protected from the top, the bird could see out.

Now I had to think of the problem of feeding. Chippy's raw beef would be too strong for a small bird still in shock, so John bought a tin of chunky dog-meat. It was no good trying to mix feathers with this for roughage, as the result was a nasty sloppy mess and difficult to handle, so I shredded up some fine white knitting wool, and used that to bind the food into manageable pieces. Then came the hard part. The owl had his beak clamped shut, and nothing was going to make him open it. After the great sledge-hammer beak of the tawny, this one was more the size of a kestrel's, fine and very sharp; and to make matters worse, it was high up, almost between those glaring eyes. Owl wriggled, Owl twisted, but Owl definitely wasn't going to cooperate in any way. I wrapped him in a small towel and laid him flat on his back between my knees. Then without getting my finger in his eyes I managed to open the beak, and with a pair of blunt tweezers inserted a tiny amount of meat and pushed it right in. Normally, as soon as food touches the back of the throat, swallowing muscles come into play, but now, as though frozen, they did not work. I dared not push harder for fear of injuring his throat with the tweezers, as it was far too small to use my finger. Only one thing to do: use another morsel to push the first one down. By that method I managed to get three pieces in, but as soon as he was put down, he bent forward and deposited the food in front of him. Oh dear! Try again. This time I managed to get some more right past the gullet, and lifting his head, with two fingers under his broad flat skull, gently eased the food along its passage in the long thin neck. I waited. The food was down. It stayed down. At this time I was more concerned with maintaining life than with actual meals, and so we persevered, little by little, every few hours. Then on the third day his throat began to work and the beak offered only token resistance. Success, and time for the owl to finish the job for himself. A little food was put on a dish by him, and he was left alone. When I returned it had all gone.

But, he had another problem. The meat was being digested and when expected results were due, being of very clean habit he would go over to the other side of the box, face the corner, and bend down to shoot his mutes away from him, then go back to his roosting corner. But what he couldn't figure out was if he had moved away, why was the roosting corner dirty when he got back? His tail feathers were in a mess, and by his look—half embarrassed, half indignant—he made it pretty plain that he didn't like it. I made him a bath out of a flower-pot saucer, put a weight in the centre like a stepping stone, half filled it with tepid water and placed it on a folded towel in a much larger box, and left him in peace with it. When I came back half an hour later the bath was empty and the little owl had preened and dried himself.

Though never having been near a human before, he gave me his absolute trust. Not once did he struggle when I had to pick him up; and I would see him watching with interest everything I did. He waited eagerly for his daily cuddle-time when he was taken from the box to snuggle up against me under the woolly jacket. For all small creatures in illness or distress, the strongest help to recovery, peace and comfort, is to be near the steady rhythmic beating of a mothering heart; and that is where the little owl wanted most to be. There he settled down happily against me. We named him Ticker.

Now that there was just a faint hope that he might be able to go free again, I was worried about him keeping his flying power, and after one of my progress reports to the vet was glad to be told that it would do no harm to let him fly. Each evening we draped the couch, bookcases and fire-place with sheets, closed the curtains, removed ornaments or anything that could be broken, and then let Ticky out. At first he ran along the floor like a little mouse, and from the corners peered out at the room while we sat quietly taking no notice of him. Then he flew. At first the weight of the splint on one leg pulled him off balance, but he soon managed to compensate for that, and made successful one-foot land-

ings on progressively higher places. But he was a bit suspicious of the quiet, and any movement would send him back to hide in a corner. Then I had the bright idea of leaving the television set switched on with the sound turned down low. That did the trick, and he spent happy times, perched like an overgrown sparrow on top of the standard lampshade, luxuriating in the warmth of the light.

After three weeks, I began to feel response from the injured foot. He was now off dog-food and on to morsels of fresh beef, was casting a good pellet regularly, and enjoyed being let out in the evenings, when he perched on the pelmet board over the curtains, completely absorbed in watching television's moving picture! He had a low undulating flight, mostly gliding from place to place, wings spread like a very beautiful moth. And the great eyes under their flat bushy eyebrows had long ago lost the expressionless snake-like stare that they first wore. Now, although not as expressive as the dark eyes of the tawny, they could show a very gentle light.

At the end of five weeks, the splint was taken off, and the vet was satisfied that all would be well once he regained the gripping power in his foot. The following day as I dressed the leg with talc to counteract itching as feathers grew again, I examined it carefully. I noticed a tiny dark patch on the pink flesh among the feathers high up on the leg. The next morning it was slightly bigger. We rushed Ticky to the surgery. The vet said that he thought it was probably bruising from the splint, but that if it were indeed infection, in such a tiny bird there was nothing that could be done. But as Ticky looked so well he was very hopeful. That evening the patch began to spread, and again Ticky asked to be cuddled. My heart sank, despite the hope that I had been given I knew that this was not bruising. That night, suddenly, the little bird slipped gently over on his side—and died.

Why, I asked myself, did he have to go through all those weeks and then succumb to secondary infection just as he was on the point of recovery? These things don't make sense. There is no knowing why.

Now he lies near that other brave little bird at the end of the garden, and my heart is both sad, and at the same time proud, that for a short space of time I was privileged to know and try to help them both. I also knew that it was probably not the last time that this would happen, but hoped that I might be given the joy of seeing the next fly back, fit and well again, to the wild night woods.

* *

And so about a month later it happened.

One evening at dusk there was a phone call for help. 'Someone has found an injured bird by the roadside. May I send him to you?' Half an hour later a very worried-looking man arrived, carefully carrying a large cardboard box.

'I've put air-holes in it as you asked,' he said, 'and a soft cloth at the bottom, because the bird won't stand up.'

We took the box indoors, and lying on its side at the bottom was a magnificent, fully grown barn owl. A female. Very gently she was lifted out. Her eyes were open, but she was still in shock and made no movement as I examined her. There was no sign of injury . . . not even a feather ruffled. She must have flown against a passing car and been knocked unconscious. Her heart was beating strongly although the pulse was rapid. Breathing was steady but fast, the eyes bright and responsive. My heart rose. Providing there was no internal injury, this bird would recover.

Again the old woollen jacket came in useful. Draping it over one shoulder and holding the owl in its comforting warmth, I sat in my chair by the fire. Gradually she recovered and moved to a more comfortable position, her feet sought for and found my arm to stand on, and her head nestled against my shoulder. After an hour or so I uncovered her to see what the reaction would be. The head slowly turned, and two intelligent black eyes studied me, showing no trace of fear or alarm. After a minute she turned, and nestling against my shoulder again, went back to sleep. John came to kneel by the chair and together we marvelled at her beauty. That such perfection of colour in white and gold, such symmetry of form and softness of feathering could exist in one creature, was a thing to take one's breath away. It was a truly wonderful thing to see. My arms were getting tired, and I thought that the time had come to put her back in the box. But the owl didn't like that idea at all, and when she found herself being placed on a wooden block there was sudden movement. Out of the box she came . . . straight back into my arms again and hid her head. So aching arms and all, I had to sit there till gone midnight and hold her. Finally, without fuss this time, she accepted the box. One foot was drawn up into her feathers, and resting quietly she spent the night by my bed.

The next day the owl slept in the semi-darkness behind closed curtains, restfully and without making a sound. At dusk, the head movements were alert and fast as she looked at me, and at the bottom of the box was a pellet. Now she would be sharp and hungry. It was time for her to go.

Near the place where she had been found we parked the car and took the box a little way into a nearby field. The owl sat on my hand, gripping my fingers tightly. I lifted her high to get a good look around. Suddenly she came to life, her claws digging strongly as she recognised her own territory. The pressure of those strong feet was the best assurance that I could have had that all was well. Calmly and without haste the big white bird took the air under her wings and went away over the fields toward some distant woods.

We have also been able to return a sparrowhawk to its freedom again. Words can't express how we felt as we watched these birds go; but we were both a bit choked up I think, because this is a very moving experience, and somehow they take something of one's own self back with them.

* *

Chippy is now five years old. He comes and goes as and when he pleases, showing that he has no intention of leaving. Even up until last spring I had hopes that he would find a mate and leave with her, but although two females have been he has turned his back on them. So now at last I am breaking my own strict rule about making pets of these owls. If he prefers to make this his home, then I can relax. In fact he started it. He seems to have turned all his attention on to us. We get landed on, sung to, and generally 'taken into his confidence'. Now he calls eagerly when he hears John's footsteps coming along the path, and when I go out, he will come winging to meet me on my return.

With Chippy in residence our work is done. Reports are coming in from areas all around: 'The owls are back again. First time in years' they say. The young from our first tawnies are spreading out to repopulate the valleys. And we are content, because we know that we are not just living in the country, but are living with the country; that vital difference which makes things the way they should be.